The Think Big Movement: Grow your business big. Very Big!

Jon Dwoskin
with A.J. Reilly

Published by Waldorf Publishing
2140 Hall Johnson Road
#102-345
Grapevine, Texas 76051
www.WaldorfPublishing.com

The Think Big Movement: Grow your business big.
Very Big!

ISBN: 978-1-945173-47-9
Library of Congress Control Number: 2016957014

Dedication

In memory of my mom and dad.
Thank you for teaching me the fundamentals, loving
me unconditionally, giving me the self-esteem to believe
there is nothing I can't do and enlightening me with your
heartfelt wisdom and all of the laughter we shared.
As you taught me, I am paying it forward.

To the love of my life and best friend, my wife Joanna.
Thank you for always listening and being by my side,
giving me your unconditional love and support, your beautiful
smile and laughter, and being the best mom in the world to our
beautiful and exceptional children, Jacob and Aria.

*One percent of all personal profits from this book will be
donated to a charity of my choice that impacts the world to be a
better place, helps in the growth of people and research and is
always: THINKING BIG!*

Table of Contents

Part One:
Successful, but Stuck

Chapter 1: Stuck

The price of discipline is always less than the pain of regret.
- Nido Qubein

The movement of the clock seemed to be slowing down. For months now, minutes were hours, hours were days, and days were weeks. Slowly creeping in was the overwhelming, suffocating feeling of being stuck. Jacob Wengrow sat at his desk watching the stock ticker flash by in one window, while another window opened to a destination far away from where he was. He tossed a golf ball in his hands, up and down, and up and down, just listening as the clock ticked on and on.

This was a special ball—his first hole-in-one—and one that he kept around for luck. It had brought luck to him that day on number 12: a short, one hundred and seventy-five yard par 3. With a flush 6-iron, Jacob watched as the ball disappeared after landing on the green. Since that day, the lucky ball had been his constant companion. He was in need of some luck now more than ever.

Fresh out of college, Jacob had started his career at Levine, Savage, and Rose Brokerage Firm. Starting from the bottom, he had labored tirelessly to climb the ladder and learn the ins and outs of this business. As he worked, he would arrive early and stay late, and through the years he had gained a strong foothold in the business. Yet, as time went on he started to see a way in which, if on his own, he could make a greater business—an enormously successful business. He began to think about the processes that LSR used to attract and retain their clients and wondered, "Is there a better way?"

Late at night he started to brainstorm, leaving the office long after his colleagues had gone home. He wrote down his ideas in a journal and continued poring over them as he had downtime throughout the day. Brokering deals started to become almost second nature to him, and he was, frankly, killing it. Tasting success for the first time in his life, Jacob wanted more. He repeatedly laid his head on his pillow at night unfulfilled from the day's work. He kept remembering what his dad used to tell him, "Success minus fulfillment equals failure."

His father had been to an Anthony Robbins' workshop and came home every night repeating this same phrase. Being a teacher was rewarding for Jacob's father, and he wanted to make sure his son understood the valuable lesson that Mr. Robbins had taught him. So, every night he'd walk through the door and repeat the same five words. Although Jacob had tasted a bit of success, because of these stinging words, he no longer felt fulfilled and needed a new plan.

As a direction formed for his new business, Jacob was ready to start his own brokerage firm. The plan was to set a new mousetrap: better ways of bringing in clients and running a company with a highly entrepreneurial culture, and targeting people who want a better, *newer* way of doing business, but were more like old souls than the current landscape of employees. His focus was to run an office that took a special interest in the client, and show them this newer, better way, ultimately endearing themselves to their clientele. Having felt deep in his heart and soul that this was the best way forward, he felt he was ready to start this new, forward-thinking, entrepreneurial endeavor. Once ready, he met with the bosses of Levine, Savage, and Rose and tendered his resignation. And, just like that, he was out on his own.

* * * *

Four years ago he had started TBM Brokerage Firm. And, like everything else in his life, it was successful at first. But, as the years passed, and the grind grew, it started to become stale. Lately, he had been complacent. He had started the company with a few clients in a bad economic climate, and from there he had grown it. As the economy improved, the clientele stayed where it was. No new accounts, no really big wins, and no answers. Jacob had done all of this on his own. As he found himself tossing his lucky Titleist Pro-V1 up and down, and up and down, he was ready to pack the clubs in the back of his car and drive out of town and off to some random place where no one knew his name.

Jacob had visions and dreams of grandeur. His plans for his business had been something in the beginning that kept him grounded. He always heard the voice of his mother or his father, who told him that there was nothing he could not do if he simply put his mind to it and believed in himself. This was a very motivating piece of advice, but in certain moments it gave him a Superman complex. It made him feel practically invincible; and, in other times (like these) it paralyzed him, leaving him searching for answers and knowing there was no one other than himself to turn to.

One of Jacob's strengths was in his ability to see down the road and plan ahead. Like any good business owner, he planned his yearly goals and, in the beginning, lived by them—eating and breathing them in as the life-source that they were. As the years passed, his visions became entrapping. His passion had formed a four-walled barrier around him that left him stuck in the monotony of the day-to-day operation of his business. And for the last year, he had his plan but was stuck in the execution of it. Sitting at his desk, staring beyond his computer screen, he thought about what Year Four had been for him.

This is just too big, he thought. He was paralyzed by the plans he had made, and in knowing that he had no direction as to how to get there.

He sat and could not bring himself to move, tossing his ball every so often, the weight of the world sitting on the shoulders of his cleanly pressed, custom-cut and monogrammed, white-cotton shirt. Jacob hated dressing up. He could not even tie his own tie until college. But, if he was going to impress the clients he was hoping to meet, but who hadn't come through the door yet, he kept up appearances. As he sat alone in his office, waiting for nothing in particular, he started to think back.

* * * *

Jacob had grown up in Metropolitan Detroit. He had grown up at the tail end of the "Bad Boys" era of the Detroit Pistons, the miserable early '90s days of the Detroit Tigers, and the mediocrity that the Detroit Lions maintained while he came of age. In a city trying to escape its failing moniker, Jacob understood the struggle of "us against the world."

Jacob's parents were never wealthy, but they were hardworking. They fought and scraped for everything they had, and from an early age, Jacob understood the value of working hard. His father was a high school history teacher and coach, while his mother worked the midnight shift at the hospital as an emergency room nurse. Though they did not have much, they did have each other: his father, his mother, his younger brother Geoff, and Jacob. The four of them were as close as they could possibly be.

A natural self-starter with a propensity for academics, Jacob breezed through middle school and high school, barely picking up a textbook to study. He particularly excelled in his math and economics classes. And, of course, he became the talk of the town when he made a nearly impossible touchdown catch in the fall of his senior year to beat the crosstown rival. He had excelled at sports, but it wasn't his forte, so eventually he headed off to the University of Michigan to pursue a degree in economics.

As time passed in college, Jacob found academics increasingly difficult. Having never truly studied in high school, he was drowning in numbers, theories, and best practices when he reached out to a fellow student, Aria, who seemed to be excelling in every class they had together. His struggle wasn't in the academic arena.

He was a smart guy, but Jacob struggled to see how any of the classes that he was paying for applied to the real life he was about to experience. Plus, he did enjoy the occasional party—much like his peers. Eventually, Jacob swallowed enough pride and found the right words to throw toward her—he didn't want her to think he had ulterior motives—and asked her to study with him.

The seeds of a blooming friendship were planted that day in Econ 201 at the University of Michigan. At the end of their college career, when Jacob's mother had passed away, it was Aria who would be by his side, holding him as he cried, and giving him the strength to face a tomorrow without the woman who had been the pillar of his existence.

* * * *

As thoughts of Aria Warren found their way to his mind, Jacob smiled for the first time in what felt like months. Aria's presence had a calming effect on him. She always had answers, almost like a savant, to the point where it would dig and dig at Jacob's ego. But in the end, she always came through, and there was no one in the world he trusted for advice more than Aria.

Tossing the trusty Titleist up into the air, Jacob thought, *how am I going to grow this brokerage? How can I execute this plan I've created?* It was a constant thought, always lurking in the back of his mind. This thought was nearly as close as his lucky golf ball. For months, it hung right there in front of his face. For all this time, he had no answer.

Like tires spinning in mud, Jacob's question just kept turning over in his mind. He had built a pretty good-sized business in four years, with at least a dozen employees, including a sales team, an administration team, and even a technology division. Everyone had his or her specific responsibilities. Jacob always took particular interest in making sure those responsibilities were done, and he held weekly staff meetings—Tuesdays at 8:00 a.m.—just to make sure that everyone was on the same page for the week. He was at the end of his rope, trying to figure out what more he could do to make his company successful and get the most he could out of his employees.

"What the hell am I gon-..." he began to ask himself.

"You ready, Jakey?" a soft, serene voice said coming from the doorway. The way the sun was setting through the windows behind her gave her a mystical glow. Not in a romantic way—that was never going to be an option—but in a sent-from-heaven sort of way. "You forgot about dinner didn't you?" Aria chided.

"Aria, hi. Um, no, I, uh, I didn't forget. Where do you wanna go? And you know I hate that name. My dad's name was Jacob. I like going by that," he corrected.

"I know. I know. Relax," she said playfully. "Come on, reservation at Cafe D'Mongo's at 7:30. You done here?"

"Haven't had anything to do for a while. Nothing more I can do tonight. I want to get out of here anyway. Let's go," he said. And with that, they were out of the office, down the elevator, and out the front door.

Another day over and no closer to a solution for this thing, thought Jacob as he smiled at Aria.

Chapter 2: Reset

I've failed over and over again in my life, and that is why I succeed. I can accept failure, everyone fails at something. But I can't accept not trying.
- Michael Jordan

As Jacob and Aria settled into the middle booth of the old speakeasy, Cafe D'Mongo's, they looked at the drink menu. There was no need to look at the regular menu because they only had two choices: ribs or chicken. Cafe D'Mongo's is a nice, quaint little restaurant that is only open Friday through Sunday and serves two items: ribs and chicken. All of the sides are the same, and the atmosphere is perfect for a Friday night getaway. That's why Jacob loved coming here. In a way, it allowed him to escape the newly formed prison that was his reality, even if only for a short time. Here, he could be someone else and forget his troubles for a while.

Tonight, with Aria, there was no escape.

"Good evening, Ma'am. Good evening, Jacob, so nice to see you again," Pauly C., the bartender, said to them as he approached the table. "Whadda-ya'll gonna have tonight?" he said, his thick accent coming out strong.

"Hey, Pauly. I'll have the ribs and a bourbon on the rocks, two green olives, please," Jacob answered.

"And for you, Miss?"

"Hi, um, I'll just take the chicken with a martini, shaken not stirred," Aria replied.

"Um, excuse me, Mr. Bond, could I have your autograph?" Jacob teased. Every time they went out it was the same exact joke, and every time Aria would just roll her eyes.

The two had kept in touch through the years after college. Luckily for Jacob, neither of them wanted to go too far from home after graduation. With his mother's passing, he was glad for a friend like Aria. Aria was thankful for Jacob, too. It was a friendship that worked, and worked well.

"How's it going, Jacob?" Aria knew the answer but asked anyway. Over the past year, she and Jacob had talked about his inability to work his plan, and how he felt trapped in a self-imposed prison.

"Eh, it's going," he responded. "Actually, Aria, I'm stuck. I'm getting up every morning, going to work, and accomplishing nothing. At least that's how it feels. My dad always said, and it keeps repeating in my mind every night, *Success minus fulfillment equals failure*. And, right now, Aria, I feel like I'm failing. Yes, I have my own business, and the business is going well, but there's no fulfillment in it. I feel trapped. I love my company, but right now it's strangling me, not sustaining me," he confessed.

"I get it," she started, "I've been where you are. Don't you remember what I was going through four years ago, right as you started TBM?"

* * * *

After graduating from the University of Michigan, Aria took a job at one of the top financial advising firms in Metropolitan Detroit. Throughout her senior year, the company had been in constant contact with her, taking her out to multiple lunches, trying to woo the girl who was among the top in her class to commit to working for them. Finally, a month before graduation, she told the partners at Kent and Rodgers Advising that she would be happy to join them.

She took a week off after school ended to move out of her dorm and into her new place, and the following Monday she began as a junior associate, with the possibility of moving up. There was a clear path to the top. There was not, however, a clear timeframe. At first, that unsettled Aria, but she eventually got used to it. At least for a couple of years.

Just like her peers, Aria had gotten restless after about two years. That upward movement she had expected was not happening. In two years, she had received just one raise; yet, her title had not changed. She imagined that things could be different on her own if she could find a new angle on the business—something that would attract people to her own advising firm. By this time, she had six reliable clients and figured that if she could get started with just these six, others would follow. How could they not? She was, of course, the top in her class at Michigan, had worked for the best, and now owned her own advising business.

Of course they will follow. We've had a good relationship for a couple of years. I'm sure they don't want anyone else handling their business, so let's go for it. She gave herself this pep talk and took the bull by the horns.

For a month before she was set to resign, she started to take her clients out to lunch. Casual, off-the-book conversations about what her (and their) futures held. She told them to take some time and think about the big decision that was before them and to let her know, giving them each a deadline of when she was set to resign. Except for the clients she had courted, which were all of her own, she seemed to drift off when it came to Kent and Rodgers business. She had mentally removed herself, a month early from it, and it was starting to concern the partners.

After a couple of weeks of long lunches and no production, they called her into a meeting. By the end of it, Aria had resigned her position—two weeks earlier than she had planned and one week earlier than the deadline she had given her clients. As she packed her things in her office, there were six numbers she made sure that she had.

She called all six of them immediately. All of the conversations could have happened simultaneously. That's how similar they were. She would start by explaining how she was transitioning earlier than expected and that she needed their answer now, along with a solid apology for making the request a full week before the date she had told them. Out of the six, five responded with the same exact message, even if the words weren't the same: they would be staying with Kent and Rodgers because they had been with them for a while, their reputation was what they paid them for, and they loved the strength and power that came from the brand that Kent and Rodgers had built, not necessarily their relationship with her. All said that she had done a great job for them. They ended the conversation with their own apology and wished her the best of luck. When they hung up, Aria was stunned. The sixth client did not answer the phone, so Aria left a message, but she expected the same answer. Now she had no idea what to do.

She had not consulted anyone about her move, nor had she planned to start from scratch, but sitting alone in her apartment, drinking her favorite glass of red wine—which was meant for celebrating, not for medication—she wondered about what the next few months would hold. She did not understand the first thing about projecting her business and didn't have a client to speak of. Yet, even starting off with certain unexpected circumstances, she pressed on. She spent eight months not earning a single penny and, ultimately, she went bankrupt.

It was her own fault really. She over-extended, did not take advice, and tried as hard as she could to make it on her own. She fell behind and was never able to catch up. Now she sat, penniless and emotionally drained, searching for answers. It was at this point that she opened herself up—and, by doing that, the entire world opened at her feet.

* * * *

Aria began to look into learning how business worked. She picked up a tape set by Brian Tracy, *The Psychology of Success*, and it began to teach her the tools she needed to be coachable, proactive, and forward thinking. She wanted to grow her business but did not have the means necessary to continue month after month with no income.

First things first, I have to make some money, she thought.

She started by taking a retail job, working only at night. She did this six days a week for the next year. This allowed her time in the morning before work to start her new financial planning business, get coaching, and have meetings with people she trusted for advice. Even with her mornings available for building her business, she was getting frazzled trying to keep it all together. On her way to a long-standing dentist appointment after a coaching webinar she had taken part in at a local coffee shop, Aria was rushing along the side of the street. Having been inundated with a ton of knowledge but not given any practical steps to accomplish these goals, a tear started to roll down her face as she thought about where this road had taken her. It was such an ambitious endeavor, yet it was poorly planned. She was working a job she had no passion for, nor any desire to go to. As she wiped a tear from her eye, steeling herself to push on, she bumped into a familiar face—one destined to bring comfort in such a down time.

"Aria?" the familiar voice asked, "funny running into you down here." It was Jacob, her old friend from college. Ashamed of her failure she had never told him the whole story. She was immediately embarrassed, wanting to turn and run as fast as possible. "Aria, it's great to see you! Wait, is everything okay? Are you crying?" Jacob asked.

"Hi, Jacob," Aria replied, scared to show her friend how upset she was, yet that desire was quickly falling from reality. She was about to lose it, and she knew it. Instinctively, she plunged herself into Jacob's chest and wrapped her arms around his waist. His arms fell to his side and then reached around her to embrace her back. Aria began to cry softly.

After a few moments of just standing there on the side of the street, Jacob finally spoke, "What's going on?" Aria hesitated at first, but eventually explained everything. If there was anyone in the world she trusted, it was Jacob. She gave him the whole story now: quitting her job—two weeks before she expected to—to start another financial planning firm, over-extending herself and her business, and the fact that she had lost everything in bankruptcy. It took all she had not to lose it completely, but like the strong individual she prided herself on being, she kept it together.

She explained that she was late for her appointment as she gave Jacob one more squeeze. As he let go, he told her that he'd call her later that evening, and that he was looking forward to getting together soon. She agreed and said her goodbyes.

Having made it to her dentist appointment on time, Aria started to feel a bit more at ease. She was now sitting in the front waiting area of MLD Dental, a place she had been going to her entire life. Dr. Marc was a face that Aria looked forward to seeing, despite him being a dentist. Dr.

Marc had a very calming presence. His graying hair now portrayed wisdom, and the glasses that sat atop his nose helped to solidify that impression. The dental assistant called Aria's name, and she took her place in the chair.

"And, how's Miss Aria this lovely afternoon?" Dr. Marc said in his usual jovial manner. It did not matter what was happening with his business or in his personal life, Dr. Marc had a warmhearted nature that set his patients at ease. His voice instantly put a smile on Aria's face. She liked being in his chair, even if it was for a teeth cleaning. As the checkup concluded without a flaw, just like always, Dr. Marc asked Aria how everything was going. Feeling a bit raw from her earlier breakdown in front of Jacob she simply said that things were going well, but did have a question for him.

"Shoot," Dr. Marc said cheerfully.

"Well, Doc," they both smirked at the Bugs Bunny reference, an inside joke from years ago, "you've built a very successful business—you've done it for what, forty years now? You seem to absolutely love coming to work each day. How do you do it? How *did* you do it?" she asked very candidly.

"Uh, um, wow … wasn't expecting that. That was very pointed. Are you sure everything is okay?"

Aria again spilled what the last ten months had looked like for her and again asked her favorite dentist, "What has made you such a success? Why do you love coming to work every day?"

"Well, Aria, it's pretty simple, to be honest. I have always wanted to be in this profession; it has been something that I've wanted to do since I was young. But passion wasn't what got me forty years in this business with a full book of clients. No, passion is good and necessary, but my success—in school and in my practice— came because of something I did a long time ago." He paused for a second, almost reminiscing, then he continued.

"Yes, when I first started in dental school at the University of Detroit Mercy, and then when I opened my practice, I knew I had to focus on two things: details and consistency with the details. I knew that if I tried to do it all, I would burn out. Then the passion I had wouldn't be enough to carry me, because Aria, passion is a desire that is fueled by success; if that fire is not continuously fueled, it slowly becomes embers of what-ifs and could've-beens. So to answer your question, I learned to focus on the small details and be very, very consistent with them. That has gone a long way to the success of MLD. I hope that answers your question."

Aria jumped from her seat, unable to contain the relief the dentist had just provided her, and simply responded, "Yes, thank you so much." Hugging the dentist she smiled at him and assured him that she would be seeing him in six months as she walked out the door. As she stepped through the threshold, the dentist called her back and gave her one more thing—his card—telling her that he was proud of the things she had been trying to accomplish and that if she ever needed anything, she should call him. Again, after another hug and a goodbye, Aria headed for the exit, on her way to focus on the details.

* * * *

At the thought of that day in the dentist's office, Aria smiled. Thinking of all she had been through, that year specifically, and where she was now, how could she not smile? Over the last three years, she had built her business by taking the advice that Dr. Marc had given her. She had started to focus on the details and consistently worked on those details, building her business over time. And now, as she sat here with Jacob, she could not help but feel the satisfaction that Jacob was clearly longing for. With this thought in mind, she looked up from the great soul food dinner she was eating in downtown Detroit and asked Jacob one question.

"Jacob, what do you want?"

"What do you mean?" Jacob quickly and confusedly responded, completely caught off guard by the question.

"It's quite simple, Jacob. What do you want? When you sit and think about your business and your life, what do you want out of all of it?" she asked, very directly. "I know that it somewhat puts you on the spot, but honestly, Jacob, it's the *biggest* question that you have to answer."

She knew this firsthand. This was the question she was asked as she was restarting her life. It was the answer to this question that got her to the point that she was at today, and she knew that Jacob probably had never thought about it before.

"I *think* that I know, but I honestly haven't really thought about that before," he responded hesitantly, knowing Aria was right. "If I'm honest with myself, the basic, fundamental desire I have is fulfillment. My father always said that *success minus fulfillment equals failure* and I don't feel like a failure, but I do not feel fulfilled. For the last year or two, Aria, I have felt like all I'm doing is spinning my wheels, stuck in the mud, and going nowhere in particular. It's a burden that feels like it gets heavier and heavier each day. I keep spinning those wheels. I don't know what the next steps are. I sit in my office, and with the light shining in through the windows, every day that light seems to grow a bit dimmer. Day in and day out."

"Okay, I understand that. I've been there," Aria said, "but you're not answering my question."

Fiddling with his fork, pulling strands of ribs from the bones and swirling it on the plate with the black beans and collard greens, Jacob finally responded.

"If I had to say right now exactly what it is that I want, it's simple: I want to come to work, build a successful brokerage firm, create a great experience for my clients, and feel the peace and joy that comes from my work. I don't want to sit at my desk and worry about the future. I want to sit at my desk, with a smile on my face, and know that I am the master of my own future."

He said this much more confidently than before. He sat back and reflected on what he had just said. After a few moments of thinking it all over, Jacob felt satisfied with his answer. He then focused his attention on Aria and asked, "How do I get to that point?"

"Well, first things first, you have to understand that this is not a quick, overnight fix. It is something that you are going to have to chase daily. You're going to have to fight for it. It is going to be something that is going to become a part of you. You have to take it to bed with you at night and put it on before your feet hit the floor in the morning. Is that something that you –"

"Yes," Jacob would not even let her finish the sentence, "more than anything, Aria, I want that, where do I start?"

Pulling her purse to the table, Aria reached into her wallet and picked out one specific business card. It was the card of Dr. Marc, her dentist. She set it on the table and grabbed her cell phone. She began to dial the number that was handwritten on the back.

As she punched the numbers, Jacob reached across the table, shielding her keypad with his hand, "You are not calling him tonight are you? On a Friday?"

"Jacob! Move your hand." She smiled, not really meaning that last part. "Dr. Marc told me that if I ever needed anything, to just give him a quick call. Seriously, he is the nicest man I have ever come across, and when I came to begin my little journey, he was the person I relied on the most, almost like a second father." She began to dial, and soon enough began to speak to the other person on the phone.

"Hello, Dr. Marc? How are you?" She waited for him to respond. "That's great to hear. Things here? Oh, they are going great. Things are definitely going well, and business is great. I have a question for you, though; I have a friend who could use a bit of advice, much like I did three years ago. Do you think you may be able to find some time to meet him for lunch or coffee?" She impatiently awaited his response and then said, "That's great! I'll let him know. Thanks, Dr. Marc." She hung up the phone and looked at Jacob with a conniving smirk on her face.

As they finished dinner, Aria filled Jacob in on the details. He was to meet Dr. Marc the following Tuesday for coffee before the workday. She gave him the number so that Jacob could contact the dentist if he needed to, and then instructed him to get back together with her and let her know how it went. After this, they went their separate ways.

Jacob's drive home was vastly different than most others. Now, for the first time in a long while, a sense of hope crept in. For the first time in forever, he had a solid feeling the satisfaction he longed for could be within reach. And now, the pursuit of that dream was about to turn into reality.

Chapter 3: When the Student Is Ready the Teacher Arrives

It is not necessary to do extraordinary things to get extraordinary results.
- Warren Buffett

Dr. Marc Gardner sat at his desk after a long day of visiting with patients and giving them the best dental care he could muster. Today was mostly checkups, but having been in the business now for forty years, even simple checkups made him tired. So, at his desk he sat, looking at his calendar for tomorrow. Tomorrow he was meeting Aria's friend, Jacob. Although he did not know the man, he was happy to help. He wanted to be available to mentor and coach anyone who would listen. With the experience he had gained over the last four decades, he felt he could help. As he looked at the calendar, he noticed in the corner of his eye a picture of him and his wife. As his focus shifted from the calendar to the frame, a silence filled the air while his mind drifted back to the happier days, before she had gotten sick.

It had not been that long since he lost his wife, though she had been sick for years. The sting of her death was not as potent as he thought it would be, but the loneliness he felt since she passed nearly suffocated him daily. This was part of the reason that he was so happy to have established a schedule so long ago that would keep him busy for much of his life. Now, in these lonely times, it helped to be surrounded by people or swimming in work. He knew that if he had time just to sit and think, his mind would go directly to her and the void that was left in his life. Sometimes, simply by reminiscing, he let himself go there; he kept this to a minimum.

As he got into the driver's seat of his car, he put the key in the ignition and pushed it forward. As he did, the radio kicked on, and the air conditioning began to blow. Over the sound of the blower, the radio was playing a familiar song: *Can't Help Falling in Love with You.* It was the rendition in its original form by The King, Elvis Presley. It was the exact song that he and his wife danced to at their wedding reception, and on subsequent anniversaries since. As tears began to well in his eyes, he turned the volume up, kept the car in park, and just listened.

* * * *

Within a period of one-and-a-half years, Dr. Marc had graduated from the dental program at the University of Detroit Mercy, opened his own practice, and married the love of his life, Barbara Creek. They had met through a mutual friend and hit it off immediately. A year later, they were married, and Dr. Marc began his dental practice: MLD Dental. Having a brand-new wife, a brand-new dental practice and a new baby on the way, Dr. Marc was thrilled with where life had taken him. With things going so well, his focus was on growing the business to support his growing family. His family was his number one priority.

Dr. Marc knew his strengths and limitations. He was a very forward-thinking dentist, even at a time when most people were not looking past today. He was one of the first dentists in the area to use a fax machine, and when computers were first finding their foothold in the world, he implemented their use in his office quickly. His colleagues thought he was insane for chasing a fad, but Dr. Marc was undeterred. From the beginning, he promised himself one thing: focus on the details and be consistent. This became the mantra by which he lived. Even with his business growing, Dr. Marc focused on how consistent he could be, day in and day out, in the midst of growth.

Five years into his business, with two young children, Dr. Marc's wife fell ill. The news was devastating to Dr. Marc, as he was feeling that the momentum he was building in his business was something that he could take to heights he had not expected. But now, those dreams of grandeur would need to be halted as he cared for his growing children and ailing wife. To Dr. Marc, there was no question as to what his number one priority would be during this time: to help his wife get better, even if this meant slowing down the effort to grow his dental practice. His focus on details and consistency was the bedrock for his transition in this situation, and it would be these principles from which he would draw day after day to survive this season of life.

Over the years, his practice had grown steadily. It never truly struggled, a testament to Dr. Marc's persistence and consistency. Not having the time to put his full effort into growing the business, he relied on one thing: his patience. For years he had plugged along, like the little engine that could, slowly growing his business and caring for those who meant the most to him.

* * * *

Waking up that Tuesday morning was effortless. Jacob's feet hit the floor the moment his alarm sounded. He quickly showered, downed a piece of toast and contemplated the day before him. Would the dentist give him a six-step process to grow his business? Would he basically hand him the keys to success and watch Jacob drive away into the oblivion with loads of cash in his hands?

The thoughts of what success looked like kept coming back to Jacob, and he smiled. Soon enough he was out the door, backing out of his parking spot, and heading to the local coffee bar ten minutes from his office.

As he walked into the coffee shop, he immediately noticed the dentist. Dr. Marc was a man in his sixties, dressed in a shirt, tie and dress pants. Even though it was standard to work in scrubs, Dr. Marc had always preferred a shirt and tie when conducting business. He was an older gentleman, with gray hair surrounding the void where the hair used to be on top of his head. He was cleanly shaven, and as Jacob walked in, he stood up and walked over to him. *This is it*, Jacob thought.

Jacob shook hands with the doctor, thanking him for meeting him so early, but quite surprised that the dentist had beaten him to the coffee shop. Jacob left and ordered a drink, then sat down in the leather chair opposite the dentist, and thanked him again.

"Jacob, there is no need to thank me. I'm happy to help in any way that I can," the dentist replied in a soft, velvety cadence. He set his newspaper on the table beside him, lifted his white coffee cup to his lips, and took a sip. "Why don't you tell me a bit of what's going on, Jacob? Let's see how I can help." He took another sip of coffee.

"Well," Jacob began, loosening his tie and sipping his black coffee, "I started my own brokerage firm four years ago, after having been in the business for a few years prior to that. I started the business to provide my clients with a different, more engaged process. At first, things went well; but lately, they have tapered off, and I just feel stuck. No fulfillment is coming out of my job, and I keep hearing my father say, '*Success minus fulfill –*'

"—ment equals failure. Tony Robbins. I love that quote. Your dad's a smart man. Why are you not experiencing fulfillment, Jacob?" It was a pointed question, but one that Jacob knew was coming.

"That's a fair question. I wish that I had some great 'wow' answer for you, but I don't," Jacob said, very sheepishly. With the feeling of hope almost vanishing as he said the words, his mood had changed. But, that was why he was here. If he was going to get help and find the fulfillment he was looking for, then it was not going to happen overnight, and it would be something that he had to work for. So he continued, "I guess, I just feel like I'm stuck in the mud, wheels spinning, and going nowhere. I had such dreams of grandeur when I first started, but since then, I have just become stuck. And, I do not know what to do to become un-stuck."

"I see," said the dentist. "Tell me, Jacob, what does a typical day look like? What is your routine?" The question was not even close to what Jacob had imagined. This was nowhere near the direction he saw the conversation going.

I figured he was going to give me the keys to the kingdom, the how to's of how to grow my business and sustain my business, and this guy is asking about my daily schedule? My routine? Jacob thought, trying his hardest not to let his face betray him before the dentist. Taking a breath, Jacob finally answered.

"I wasn't expecting that question, sorry. Let me think," Jacob began, then continued to discuss his morning and mid-afternoon schedule, ending with, "but really it depends on the day." Jacob felt as if he impressed the dentist when he smiled at the answer that he was given.

"That right there. That's what I was waiting to hear." Dr. Marc smiled as he began explaining himself. "You said, *it just depends on the day*. You know what that tells me? You are run by your schedule and to-do list, rather than mastering it yourself. My practice was at a slow, nearly snail's-pace growth; but that was not because I planned it that way, but because I was forced into growing it at such a slow pace. Five years into my practice, when things were really starting to pick up, my wife became ill. Her health and the well-being of my family became my focus, but I knew that I could not just give up the business, so I focused on smaller things that I could do every day, consistently, that would lead to exponential growth over time. Small investments of time that would eventually pay huge dividends. But, do you know what the key was?"

Here was the moment Jacob was waiting for. The moment when all his problems would be answered, where he would find the secret recipe that would lead to fantastic growth, and along with it would come success and fulfillment. He could barely contain his excitement. "What was the key, Dr. Marc?"

"Consistency."

"What?" Jacob's giddiness was turning to suspicion at such simplicity.

"Consistency. 'Firmness of constitution or character; substantiality; durability; persistency. His friendship is of noble make and a lasting consistency.' From the fourth definition of Mr. Webster. It shows us, Jacob, that consistency is a characteristic of your character that is of utmost importance. How can one be trusted with great success if they cannot handle the smallest of tasks? The goal, for you and me, in order to build our business is consistency. But along with consistency, you have to master your planning; there is no such thing as winging it. You've heard the story of the turtle and the hare, no?"

Jacob smiled, confused by the example Dr. Marc had given him. "The turtle and the hare, the old children's story?"

"That's the one. Remember it? The hare challenges the turtle to race, and when the starting gun fires, the hare shoots out for a massive lead. But, because of his arrogance and the lead that he establishes early on, he eventually stops by the side of the track—he gets sidetracked, as it were—and is no longer doing what he's supposed to be doing. Meanwhile, the turtle just keeps plugging along, *consistently*, doing exactly as he should. And who won the race? The turtle, Jacob; Mr. Consistency. Be the turtle, Jacob, if you want to grow your business. Anyone can gimmick their way into growth that isn't sustainable; but the wise man learns how to consistently grow his business."

Jacob pondered the analogy, wondering how he could implement this consistency Dr. Marc talked about. What were the things he needed to do in order to do them consistently? He looked over the edge of the coffee cup he was sipping from to the face of Dr. Marc, whose gaze had wandered to other parts of the shop. Dr. Marc wore a smile of pure satisfaction, not because he had just schooled Jacob, but the kind of pure satisfaction that comes solely from enjoying every facet of your life. It was the type of smile Jacob had been longing for, and now he felt one step closer to finding it.

With that, Jacob thanked Dr. Marc for his time, and the dentist responded, "I like you, Jacob. At my age, it's not every day that you get to meet someone new. I tell ya what, I'll coach you, mentor you, help you through whatever it is that is going on as your journey down this road begins. I'm going to send you to various people that I know, each of whom will give you different pieces of advice they have learned as they began their own businesses. Come back to me once a month; we'll meet together and we'll conquer this thing, Jacob, just you wait and see.

"The first person I want you to contact is my friend, Sharon Potts. She is an artist who pushed her way through discouragement. She'd be a great person for you to talk to."

The dentist gave Jacob Sharon's number, shook his hand, and was out the door.

Chapter 4: Finding Your Passion

The biggest risk is not taking any risk. In a world that's changing really quickly, the only strategy that is guaranteed to fail is not taking risks.
- Mark Zuckerberg, Facebook founder

On his way to the office, Dr. Marc called Sharon Potts.

"Hey Sharon, how's the art business?" He was just warming her up for what came next. After a few more minutes of catching up and small talk, Dr. Marc said, "Say, I just met a guy; young, ambitious, smart, but ultimately discouraged with his business right now. I gave him your number to contact you. That's alright, isn't it?" Sharon agreed that it was and they both hung up the phone.

Sitting in her studio apartment, Sharon gazed through the sunlit room toward one of her works of art— a single charcoal drawing hanging next to an open window. It was on a smaller canvas, 11 inches by 14 inches. Yet, even across the room she couldn't help but look at the work and smile. It was a type of portrait, and the subject was someone she knew quite well. She had done the drawing after a very trying time in her life—a time when she almost gave up her art. She entitled the work, *Passion,* and as the wind blew in through the window, Sharon was reminded of the day she created that picture.

* * * *

Sharon Potts had always loved art. From the time she was in pigtails as a young girl, she loved to draw, even getting in trouble by plastering her works of art in crayon all over the bathroom walls. She caught a bit of trouble for it, but it didn't slow her down.

As she got older, she continued to develop her love for art, dabbling in any form she could find the necessary materials for. She painted, sketched, sculpted, and even tried her hand at a little graffiti. Whatever it took for her to create, that's what she wanted to do. She especially loved creating pieces that she could hang in her house and decorate her space with. Every wall of her studio apartment had her very own work on it. The thought of selling her work never came to mind. She didn't need money.

For five years now, she had been by herself. Ever since the day she got the phone call that changed her life.

She had met and married Steve Potts ten years ago. It was one of those classic love-at-first-sight-married-within-a-year type romances. He was a very sought-after, nationally-known brain surgeon who provided Sharon the opportunity to create her art and fill their home with her masterpieces. Five years into the marriage, while she was at home working on another piece to hang in their guest room, she received a phone call.

"Hello?" Sharon said.

"Mrs. Potts? This is Dr. Allen Greenway; I need you to come to Metropolitan General. It's your husband, Steve." Shocked, distraught, and unable to move, Sharon slumped to the ground. "Mrs. Potts, are you there?" Dr. Greenway called to her.

"Y-Y-Yes, sorry. What happened? Is Steve okay? Oh God, if something happened to hi—" her words began to run together as she frantically tried to make sense of the information being given to her.

Dr. Greenway immediately cut her off, "Ma'am, it's best you get down here quickly. Your husband has had a stroke. He's on a breathing machine now, but that will only give him enough breath for you to say goodbye. I beg you, please hurry."

With that, she threw on her coat and headed to the hospital, trying to face the fact that today would be the last time she saw her husband in this lifetime.

After burying Steve, Sharon did the only thing she knew how to do to cope with the tragedy of such a loss: create art. She drew, and painted, and sculpted, self-medicating herself with her art, rather than a more destructive option. She poured herself into her art, day in and day out. Steve had left her in a position, through his work and life insurance, that she did not need to work to support herself. She did, however, in a more financially responsible decision, sell their house and move into a much cheaper, more artfully appropriate studio apartment. She spent her days losing herself and her emotions in the art that she created.

* * * *

Five years after the death of her husband, Sharon Potts still missed him every day. The last years had not been easy, but she had made it. And, she even had begun to sell her art. She had become very accustomed to her surroundings: the modest studio in Detroit with her very own creations lining the walls.

On the anniversary of Steve's death, she decided to host a party for friends and family to help keep her mind off of what the day represented, but also, to honor the life Steve had given her.

That Thursday night, by 7:00 all the guests had arrived, nearly twenty of them, at her top-floor dwelling. It was a beautiful fall evening and in order to create more room for her guests she opened the large sliding glass door that led to the balcony. The view from her Carlton Lofts apartment gave her and her guests a stunning view of some older houses, Ford Field, a night game at Comerica Park, and, in the distance, the beauty of a fully lit Renaissance Center.

The wine was flowing, people were congregating, and a select few were on the balcony enjoying a nice cigar she had picked up from the Pages Cigar Lounge, the shop belonging to her husband's longtime tobacconist, Adam Sullivan. In fact, she noticed that one cigar was sitting amongst those the guests lit, but it was seated on the edge of an ashtray with no one laying claim to it. She smiled when she saw it. Her husband had done the same thing when his father had passed. One last smoke with an old smoking comrade.

As the night wore on, Sharon was approached by a longtime friend, Susan Sheridan. The quickness and giddiness that Susan approached Sharon with caught her off guard, giving the impression that Susan was having quite the time.

"SHARON! Sharon, what a lovely party!" Susan said through her Merlot-stained teeth.

"I'm so glad you're enjoying yourself," Sharon responded.

"I am. I am. I was just telling Don how wonderful your decorative art was. Simply beautiful."

"Thank you, I do them all right here, staring out that window. Ever since Steve passed," she paused for a moment and thought about her husband, "it has been my way of coping. I paint, or draw, or sculpt and then find the perfect place around the apartment for them."

"Have you ever sold a piece?" Susan said, a bit forward for the occasion.

"No. Not one. Haven't even tried," Sharon responded.

"Well there is a particular piece hanging in your bathroom that I'd love to have. Would you sell it?"

"What one are you talking about?"

"The one with the children playing, vibrant colors splashed throughout the background. It's a very happy piece, one that I would love to hang in my sitting room. How much could I give you for it? Four hundred dollars?"

"Susan, that's a lot of money for a no-name artist."

"I won't hear of it, if you'll take the money, I'll take the painting. You really should think about selling your pieces; they are wonderful."

"I guess I could do that," Sharon said, hesitant as she was; the only works that had left the apartment were her quarterly donations she had made to the Boys and Girls Club for their yearly charity auction.

"Sharon, you should consider selling your work. I know you live comfortably, but you could really make some serious extra income. Do what you want, hon, but I think you have something here."

Sharon paused and thought about the possibility, unsure of where to begin. But Susan persisted and suggested that she should continue to sell pieces, and could even be commissioned for any work someone wanted from her.

"Think of what a business that could be!" she exclaimed. Sharon agreed, and the next day began putting the wheels in motion to begin selling her art.

Within four years, Sharon's business, From the Heart, had been more than she had bargained for. She was doing very well and was very busy, but she had lost the grip on why she loved art in the first place. Originally, she had used art as an expression of her emotion, something that was essentially a part of who she was. She would display these pieces all over the apartment and could look at any work and remember the effort, emotion, and time that were strewn from each brushstroke.

Now, as she was being commissioned to paint someone else's landscapes or someone else's mural in their child's nursery, her art had grown to the point where she no longer was fulfilled in her work, nor satisfied with the outcomes. After four years of a decrease in her enjoyment and fulfillment, she sat alone in her dark apartment one night and began to cry.

"Is this all there is to my life now?" she wondered. The feeling of guilt began to creep into her thoughts as she nursed a glass of pinot noir and blankly stared through the sliding glass door overlooking the Detroit skyline. She couldn't help but feel like she had let herself down. She didn't need the money, but the thought of other people enjoying her work did give her a sense of encouragement.

"People do not have to pay me money to enjoy my work. And, really, is the work I've been doing 'my work?' It isn't. It is what other people want me to create, not something I am inspired to paint. Art was my passion, a piece of me. Now it has become a job."

In that moment a thought of clarity sprang into her mind. She quickly got up from her patio couch, and rushed into her apartment, grabbing a small 11-inch by 14-inch canvas. She sat it upon her easel and began to work. The only muse she needed that night was the reflection in the long sliding glass door. As she removed the charcoal from its resting place, she began again to draw. This time the subject was herself, sitting at her workstation, creating what would become known simply as *Passion*.

* * * *

Jacob was so enthusiastic after his meeting with Dr. Marc that it did not take him a full day to call Sharon. He worked, barely able to focus, but nevertheless was very productive. He looked for details he could implement into his daily routine, consistently, trying to do as Dr. Marc said right from the beginning. He didn't know why, but for some reason he trusted Dr. Marc more than he trusted anyone at the moment. There was something about him: his charisma, his sage demeanor that just made Jacob feel at ease right away. He knew that the journey to a successful business and fulfillment would begin with the dentist he just met. Now, his first task was to call Sharon Potts.

Jacob stayed a bit later in the office that night. After all his calls to clients and meetings were done for the day, he got out the number for Mrs. Sharon Potts and dialed. Sharon picked up and Jacob introduced himself.

"Hi ma'am, my name is Jacob Wengrow, and I was given your number by Dr. Marc Gardner. I have been discussing my business with him, and he gave me your number and said that you could help me a bit. I know that it is out of the blue, and I'm sorry if I have caught you at a ba—"

"Honey, he told me you'd be calling. Please don't go apologizing all over yourself," Sharon replied, excited to have the opportunity to chat with a young, ambitious businessman, in a way that reminded her of her late husband.

"Well, ma'am, I'm just getting to know him. We've only had coffee just once. A close friend recommended him to me. I am looking for some help, and I heard he's the guy to turn to," Jacob responded.

"Well, that's good to hear. Marc and I go back a long way. In fact, when I was struggling with the business I was running, he was who I turned to. He was always such a gentleman, such a wise man, and I truly am thankful for the way he came alongside my discouragement and helped me through it."

"That's actually why I am calling you," Jacob said. "It seems that I have been fighting the wind in my own business and I reached out to Dr. Marc, who gave me some advice and turned me to you. Do you think you may be able to help me?"

"Absolutely, sweetheart. If Marc recommends you, there's no way I can say no," she responded with an enthusiasm Jacob didn't expect. She continued on to tell Jacob of the ups and downs of her own attempt to enter the business world, how she loved creating her own works, but the hustle of the day in and day out had robbed her of the joy she felt in her creations. "It was really tough," she said.

"How did you handle that?" Jacob replied, curious because he had felt the things she was describing. "I sometimes feel like all I'm doing is spinning my wheels and getting nowhere. I dread the days when I cannot get ahead. It's discouraging, to say the least. Especially when things started so well," Jacob confided.

"Honey," said Sharon, quietly and calmly across the phone line, "when I sold my first piece of art it was an adrenaline rush, a real experience. Eventually, though, working and creating on someone else's inspiration and dime completely took all the joy out of my work. The pieces of art that had once been a part of me, something I created, were just extra. Like that little bit of hangnail when you've cut your fingernails too short. It's there only as a reminder of a mistake, and it's painful. I just could not do it any longer. So I stopped."

"You just quit?"

"Oh, heavens no! I can't quit my art. It is as much a part of me as the red hair on my head or the green eyes in my face. I will never be able to step away from my art; but, I did stop working for other people."

She continued, "I started finding my muse in everything I experience through the day, and that is what I drew, not what others asked me to draw. Then the fires of passion began to rekindle, and now they burn intensely, day in and day out. Let me ask you, Jacob, what are you passionate about?"

The silence on the other line seemed to last for a decade, and eventually she spoke again, "Are you passionate about what you do? Not only are you passionate about it, but are you *obsessed* with it?"

"I am," Jacob interrupted, "I absolutely love what I do. When I first started TBM Brokerage, I couldn't stay in bed and went full gusto toward the finish line. But as the years passed, and the clients weren't lining up at my door, it became cumbersome. Even though it weighs on me every day, there is nothing else I'd rather be doing. I love the people I work with, and I love the work. I could say I'm obsessed with it."

"That's good, honey, that's good." He could hear her smile through the phone. She continued, "When you have a unique talent, you have to chase that ferociously all the time. You have to do what you love and do what is seared on your soul. But the key is you have to do it for no one else but yourself. That is the key, Jacob. I hope that helps."

It did. It wasn't a long call, but it was long enough. They had never met, but he felt like he'd known her forever. In just a few short moments, she had rekindled something inside of him. He did love what he was doing. He was obsessed with it, which is why he struggled so much with not succeeding. But now, with this reminder of how much he loved what he was doing, he was ready. Ready to again rekindle that fire of passion with TBM and charge into a successful future.

"One more thing, sweetie," the soft voice from the other end of the phone line added, "I've got someone to add to your list. He's a great friend and a confidant of my late husband. Tomorrow after work, I want you to visit Pages Cigar Lounge. It's down near Campus Martius. Ask for the owner, Adam Sullivan. He'll help you on this journey. And, while you're at it, you can grab a nice cigar."

Jacob smirked but liked the thought of lighting up a Nicaraguan puro. It had been a while since he had something like that to look forward to.

Chapter 5: Balance

The successful warrior is the average man, with laser-like focus.
- Bruce Lee

As Jacob hung up the phone, a sudden sense of overwhelming doubt pervaded the space around him. Like the dark knight waiting in the wings, stalking his prey, a cloud of darkness began to move towards Jacob. He had only truly just begun his journey. *I can't already be discouraged*, he thought. He reached into his pocket to grab his lucky golf ball, which always seemed to do the trick of calming him down, but noticed emptiness where it always lay. In the excitement and concentration he had devoted to his conversation with Sharon, he must have walked out of the office without his lucky Titleist.

"Dammit!" he whispered to himself. He walked to his dry bar, grabbed the bottle of bourbon and poured himself a glass. Two rocks, one finger. Just enough to take the edge off.

He threw himself into a rarely used lounge chair, which sat opposite an even more rarely used couch in his living room. It was one of those chairs that had a higher back, so when Jacob sat down, his arms were resting in a near ninety-degree position from his body. He didn't mind this though. It was a perfect resting place for his drink. Jacob grabbed his phone and dialed Aria's number.

"Hey Jacob," she answered.

"Hey Aria, you got a second?"

"Sure do. Was just hopping into the shower before bed, but I can talk. What's up?" she wondered.

Jacob caught himself smiling and was appreciative of the kind gesture, something he could always rely on from his oldest college friend.

"Is everything okay, Jake?" she prodded.

"Huh? Yeah, yeah. Everything is fine. Just got off the phone with Sharon Potts, a lady recommended to me by Dr. Marc."

"And ..."

"She was sweet as could be. Seriously, I've never been given so many nicknames in my entire life. But it was what she said that hit home for me. Aria, this woman doesn't work. She told me all about why she didn't have to work, and how she was able to create her art whenever she felt like it. She seemed very free. I guess she was in business once and had been pretty successful, although when she talked, you could almost hear a sort of pain in her voice as she talked about when she actually sold her art."

Aria, on the other end of the phone, knew what Jacob was thinking and feeling. Sharon Potts had played an integral role in her development too, so she just let Jacob talk.

"She talked to me about passion, Aria. Passion. She said that each piece of her art is a part of who she is, and when she was working and being commissioned by other people, those pieces weren't a part of her. They just were 'something extra, like a hangnail,' if I remember correctly."

"So, what is the problem —?" Aria asked.

"It wasn't an epiphany that I'm in the wrong line of work. Nothing like that. I absolutely love what I do. There's joy in it, just not lately. For a year or so now –"

"Jacob," she interrupted, "slow down, you've just begun talking with Dr. Marc, and you've talked to him, what, once? You need to relax, just a bit. This change isn't something that is going to occur overnight, and it is something that is going to create moments like tonight where you start to freak out. And I don't mean this badly. Not at all! Who did Mrs. Potts tell you to meet next?"

"Adam Sullivan," Jacob responded, noticing a bit of laughter on the other line. "What, what is it? I know I didn't say something funny, so what the hell are you laugh_"

"Stop. Chill out, Jacob." Aria stopped him in his tracks. "I laughed because Sully is one guy, especially after this conversation, that you *must* talk to. Finish your bourbon and go to bed. Tomorrow, get ahold of Adam. I bet you will enjoy what he has to say."

They both hung up the phone. Jacob now was more curious than he was worried.

* * * *

Adam Sullivan turned the lamp off on his desk, packed up his leather bag, and turned the lights off in his classroom. His destination tonight was not his home after work, but to his second home, and his second career. During the school year, Adam pulled double shifts on three out of five days during the week and worked nearly every weekend. He taught literature at the local high school in Ann Arbor. Being a teacher meant he needed extra income. He didn't want his wife working, so she was able to pursue other passions she had.

A few years back—five to be precise—he ventured out into his own business and started Pages Cigar Lounge. It was the perfect culmination of his English teaching profession and his love of nice cigars.

Adam had started Pages five years ago, kicking off the business during his summer vacation. He had dabbled in other lines of work during his previous fifteen years as a teacher, but all of them ended the same way: him frustrated, never getting ahead, and generally grumpy. He and his wife sat down the night before school six years ago and just discussed the future, knowing they could not keep at the current pace and survive. That's when he laid plain his desire to start his own business—something that, since he had to work two jobs, he would enjoy being a part of rather than despising. And, on that August date, Pages Cigar Lounge was born.

The first five years were good. Not great, but they were sustainable. It just meant that his workdays were a bit longer, especially during the school year. He thought that he had the perfect setup for a great cigar shop, too. Being as well-versed in literature as he was, given his day job, he set up a library-type atmosphere with books lining the walls of his shop. Naturally, there were televisions too, but he wanted to make sure that if guys or girls wanted to come in and enjoy a cigar and read a book, they had every opportunity to do that. He had a steady clientele, a couple of good employees who he trusted, and a business that was running quite smoothly.

There is something nice about doing things that you love. His problem came when he had to sacrifice time with his family to make this work. At first, much of his time was spent at the shop, and it started to wear on his wife and boys. After two years of constant working, he and his wife had to devise a plan in order to balance their lives. The balance was their key, and balance was their goal. They loved the life they had created and, after their initial talk of balance, had put all their efforts towards it. For three years now, because he was doing what he loved and his family was taken care of, Adam was as content as he had ever been.

* * * *

Jacob left work early on a Friday afternoon and took the forty-five-minute drive to Adam's cigar shop. He enjoyed cigars and was happy to meet a fellow lover of the leaf. He was more excited about what Adam could offer his business, especially after his little conversation with Aria the night before. He parked on the street and walked through the front door of Pages Cigar Lounge, immediately overtaken with the smell that reminded him of his grandfather. It was a nostalgic smell that brought a smile to his face.

There's something to be said about an establishment that is designed purely for relaxation and enjoyment. For most, this might be at the hands of a masseuse or maybe in the soft cushion of a nicely broken-in reading chair with a gripping tale of adventure. For some, however, it is found in the blended tobacco leaves of their favorite cigar, toasted just perfectly, while the cares of the day melt away over the next hour to ninety minutes. This last experience was what Jacob was looking forward to the most.

Jacob entered the cigar store and was immediately overtaken by the ambiance. The first thing he noticed was the wooden Indian chief that greeted him as he crossed the threshold. He looked to his left and gave a nod to the old chief, knowing the symbolism attached. Since nearly the inception of the Jamestown colony, tobacco has been a staple product in America. Thus, the Native American came to represent something of an advertisement for tobacco shops. If you saw the old wooden chief, back in the day, you knew the store sold tobacco.

Jacob was greeted by a mid-sized man with a round face, equally round glasses and thinning salt-and-pepper hair, roughly combed to the left side of his head.

"Sir, how are ya doing today?" the man asked.

"I'm well," Jacob responded, as the man approached and extended his hand for a courtesy handshake. The intimate customer service caught Jacob off guard, but immediately set him at ease.

Jacob continued to look around, noticing the shop was divided into two areas: the front had a couple of televisions, couches and leather chairs. Some were arranged in a communal fashion, and all, of course, facing the entertainment. The PGA golf tournament of the week was on one, and the Tigers game on another. In front of each, a smattering of customers sat and enjoyed their various cigars and beverages. The second area in the shop was quiet and secluded, towards the back of the establishment. It was set up like a library, and the name of the place began to make sense.

"Is there anything I can help you find today?" asked the gentleman who had warmly greeted Jacob.

"Yes, actually, two things. First, a lady named Sharon Potts sent me here. She told me to look for the owner, Adam. Do you know where I can find –"

The man cut him off, "Sharon Potts! She told me you'd be stopping by. Adam Sullivan. Nice to meet you, Jacob. I'm assuming that second thing you were going to ask for was a cigar?"

They caught each other's eyes and they both smiled at how obvious the question was. Jacob immediately felt comfortable with Adam, the seemingly outgoing owner and operator of Pages Cigar Lounge.

"Sharon and I, well more her husband, Steve, go way back." Adam continued, "He and I used to get together quite often many evenings and share a smoke. That guy loved his cigars. We sure do miss him around here."

"Sharon didn't share much with me about him, and I didn't want to pry."

"Steve was a great guy, and they were great together. It's a shame how suddenly he left. Way too early. Since then Sharon and I have stayed in contact; in fact, she would always talk to me about her business, and when I was going to start this place, she was one of the people I went and talked to about being in business for yourself. I'm assuming that's how you two met?"

"Yes, sir."

"Son, my father is 'sir.' Please just call me Adam. I may be a bit older than you, but in here we're all on the same playing field. Now, what do you like to smoke?"

"It's been a while since I've had a cigar, to be honest. I've been so busy lately. Late hours at the office and all. I just haven't made the time to actually enjoy one," Jacob confided.

"Well, that ends tonight. Mild, medium, or full strength?" Adam asked to gauge the type of cigar he could suggest for his new friend.

"Nothing that's too strong, that's for sure. How about something medium body, with some good flavor? Maybe a good, solid, Nicaraguan blend."

"Great," Adam said, "follow me." He opened the door to the humidor for Jacob and motioned for him to follow. They stood before over one hundred facings of cigars, as Adam's eyes scanned the shelves. In the humidor, the sounds of the television were drowned out, but the smooth stylings of Count Basie and His Orchestra were being piped in through the overhead speakers. Jacob loved jazz, and with each passing moment, he felt more and more at home in this place.

"Pick one out for me, Adam, I'll completely trust your judgment," he said.

Adam reached into a box of cigars and picked out one that was perfectly situated on the shelf. "Here you go. The 1964 Padron Anniversario Exclusivo. One of the finest cigars on the market: a Nicaraguan puro, which means that all the tobacco comes from Nicaragua. With a beautifully crafted Habano wrapper."

"Great, I'll take it," Jacob said.

"Let's get you all set up here." Adam reached into his pocket, grabbed his twin-blade cigar cutter, neatly clipped off just enough of the cap to allow air to pass, and handed the cigar to Jacob.

Jacob took it in his hands and made his way back to the counter looking for the torch lighter to get the thing started. He grabbed the lighter, held the cigar between his thumb and first two fingers, pointing the foot away from him and toward the lighter. He remembered that he needed to toast the edges of the wrapper first, then work toward the middle, ultimately achieving that bright, cherry glow. Once he was set, he took a seat next to Adam, and the two of them began to talk.

* * * *

As both men sat and enjoyed their cigars, Jacob remembered how much he had enjoyed this particular activity, and wondered why he had gone so long between sticks. He was pleasantly surprised by how easily the conversation flowed between the two of them.

"When did you start Pages?" he asked.

"Five years ago. I teach as my first career. High school English. But, my wife and I had come to the same conclusion that we would prefer if she didn't work. That way our kids could have the support they needed, whenever they needed it. Problem was, losing her income would not set us up to be financially comfortable. So, in order to supplement my meager teaching income, I ventured into different odds-and-ends jobs, picking up work to support her staying home and chasing her dreams. At first, I started to deliver newspapers early in the morning at the airport. I was up by 3:30 every morning, making my rounds to all the convenience shops in the various terminals. Then I was gone by 7:00 and off to school. You want to talk about tired? Teaching takes it out of you as it is, but add to that a fifteen-hour per week job *before* teaching, and that's the catalyst for the creation of a grumpy old man. And I was. So I left there and went to work at Walmart every other night, including weekends. This was a bit better, but it took me away from my family at night, including Little League games and parent-teacher conferences. I'm telling you, it is nearly impossible to live on a single income these days."

"So where does Pages fit in?" Jacob asked, openly admiring the care and devotion Adam had for his family.

"Well, that's the thing. About six years ago, I was spent. I was running on fumes, and barely spending time with my family, let alone being able to enjoy a cigar when I wanted to. My wife, the wonderful woman that she is, told me that I needed to stop running myself into the ground, that she had enjoyed being my wife to this point, but if I kept this up, I wouldn't be around long enough to see my children grow. That woke me up. She called her uncle, Marc Gardner –"

"Wait, you're Marc's nephew?" Jacob sprung forward.

"Well, nephew-in-law. How do you know Marc?"

"Long story, but essentially he is my friend's dentist. He helped her with her own business, so when I started struggling she set me up with him. He directed me to Sharon, and Sharon sent me to you. We met last week for coffee, and I guess he liked me enough because he suggested taking me under his wing as a mentor."

"Ha! Uncle Marc – always the mentor!" Adam smiled to himself.

"He's one of the wisest men I have ever met, you'll do well to listen and soak in whatever it is he directs you towards. Anyway, my wife called Uncle Marc and set up a time for the two of us to go golfing one Saturday morning. While we trekked back and forth across the golf course, he suggested that I go into business for myself. He simply asked, 'Adam, what is it that you love to do?' I told him that I loved what I was doing as a teacher, but needed to make more money, and that I also had an affinity for cigars. We tossed around the idea of combining the two, and Pages was born in my mind that day. I went home with an excitement I hadn't had in years and told my wife, who surprisingly supported the idea right from the get-go."

"Wow. But starting your own business. That had to be more demanding of your time than the other two jobs you worked?" Jacob asked.

"It was, no question about it. We decided to give it one year, to save as much as we could, get the business plan in order—under the direction of Uncle Marc, of course—and still had to take out a small loan. But, five years ago Pages came into existence. That first year I did everything. Had to. If I was busy when I worked jobs I didn't care about, starting this business was ten times busier. But now I was doing something that I enjoyed. The problem was, after one year I could still see the wear and tear it was creating at home, and my wife and I sat down to have another talk."

"Did she want you to get out?" inquired Jacob.

"No, no. She's always supported me, but she wanted me around. I get that. We haven't really discussed your business, but for me, this is the advice that I should give you: find balance. Balance is the key to any successful and happy life, marriage, or business. When things are out of balance, nothing goes right. When you strike that balance, happiness soon follows," responded Adam.

"How did you find the balance?" Jacob asked, laughing to himself. He recalled Aria's words the night before, *Sully is one guy, especially after this conversation, you must talk to.* She was right.

"It's not easy. Balance takes sacrifice. I had to re-examine my approach to this business; how could I make it effective and at the same time throttle down? I put myself on a schedule, hired employees, and a manager, Tom Smith. Old Tommy saved my backside. The most dependable guy I know, I trust him completely. He and my employees do a great job, and they do well covering for me, so I don't have to miss any more family events. Hell, I even got the chance to coach my kids' Little League team this year. Some of the most fun I've had in a long time.

"No matter where you are at with your business, Jacob, remember this: find a balance. I'm sure Uncle Marc gave you the talk about details, right? Details are huge. Work those details and don't give up on them, but while you're working those details, find balance. Find balance my friend." He smiled and patted Jacob on the back.

Both men finished their respective cigars, Jacob shook his hand and thanked Adam for his time. He ended by asking Adam what he owed for the cigar, and Adam simply told him, "This one's on me." Jacob enthusiastically thanked him, then headed off to find balance.

Chapter 6: The Epiphany

The dream is free. The hustle is sold separately.
- Anonymous

Jacob's mind was racing early the next morning as all this advice swirled through his head. He never set the alarm on Saturday mornings. These mornings were his to enjoy the relaxing comfort of his king-sized bed with plush, Egyptian cotton sheets. But, on this Saturday morning, he was restless.

Marc had told him that it was all about the details, consistency, and planning. Sharon advised him to only work for his passion. Adam had shown him that balance in his life was the only way that he could begin to feel fulfilled with his workload.

As he lay awake, tossing back and forth, he eventually gave up trying to sleep, and slipped his feet into his morning slippers. Dressed only in his white Jockey v-neck he wore the day before and his blue cotton boxers, he shuffled into the kitchen. Still skirting the line between dreams and reality, he finally made it to the coffee maker. He filled the carafe with water, emptied out the day-old coffee, and reached for a new filter. There were none. With a what-a-way-to-start-the-day eye roll, he walked back to his bedroom where he threw on a pair of jeans, tennis shoes, and a Tigers ball cap. He grabbed his keys and headed for the door. He knew that the Starbucks a block away would give him the chance to sit and take in his caffeine in relative solitude. Just in case, he made sure to bring his ear buds with him.

It won't be that bad. I can listen to some good jazz, and catch up on any news I may have missed this week, he thought to himself as he headed toward the coffee goddess and the caffeinated blessings that awaited him.

The line was not too long when he arrived; it was the first thing that had gone right for him this morning. Approaching the counter, Jacob ordered a venti dark roast, grabbed a *New York Times*, and found a comfy chair to sink into. His white cup with brown cardboard sleeve instinctively was placed on the table to his right. He was seated by the wall, with his little table on his right just where he liked it, and another chair uncomfortably close on his left with its own table to its left. He opened the paper to the Current Events section and began reading. He only got to the second paragraph when a large shadow appeared directly in front of him. He slowly allowed his eyes to move upwards in the direction of the shadow. He couldn't help but notice that he was in the presence of someone who looked like an NFL linebacker.

"Excuse me, buddy, is this seat taken?" the man asked Jacob.

"Nope, not that I know of," Jacob replied, as he removed an ear bud from his left ear.

"Great!" the big man said boasting a smile at the same time. Then he plunged down into the chair, forcing it back a few inches under his mass. "Gee, guess they don't make these things that sturdy," he said, trying to engage Jacob in a conversation he preferred not to be a part of.

"Nothing's made like it used to be," was the only response that Jacob could come up with. Not his best work, but short and to the point in the hopes that the guy would take the message. The gleeful giant with wide shoulders was sitting insanely close. He turned toward Jacob and extended his hand. He had to bend his elbow just to keep it from extending all the way across Jacob's entire body.

"The name's Michael Paige."

Jacob noticed the extended paw almost dwarfed his entire chest. He shared his own name and shook the man's hand, also noticing that his own was lost inside Michael's.

"Beautiful day. Great day for a coffee and good company," Michael said.

Jacob now realized that he was trapped in the stranger's conversation and there was no escape. Then Michael asked for the sports section, "If it isn't too much trouble." Jacob seized the opportunity to occupy his new guest with a different focal point, hoping to return to his seclusion. He handed the sports section to Michael and was promptly thanked.

"Great time of year," Michael began, "what with the baseball season wrapping up, the Tigers in the hunt, football only a couple weeks away, and the Red Wings right after that. Could there be a better time to be a sports fan? You a sports fan, Jacob?"

"Yes, but lately I've just been too busy for anything other than work. Which is why I came here to read up on what I've missed." As pointed and truthful as it was, Jacob wasn't expecting to be this candid, but Michael's easy, casual acquaintance seemed to have this effect on him. He was clearly one of those people who captivate you from the first word. Yes, this was exactly Michael Paige.

"I get it," Michael responded. "What is it that you do?"

"I own my brokerage firm, TBM Brokerage. Started it a few years ago, and over the last few years have been spinning my wheels trying to find fulfillment in what I'm doing." Jacob cut himself off; he was usually not as open as he was being in this moment.

"I've been there. I played linebacker at Michigan State University about twelve years ago." Jacob immediately nodded, the size of this guy finally making sense.

"My senior year, I was projected as a top ten pick in the draft for the following spring. Then, in my final game against the Buckeyes, I went to make a tackle right up the middle on a dive play, and one of their linemen doubled back and clipped me with a dirty block. Broke my leg in two spots below the knee and ended my career that day. Millions of dollars gone in about three or four seconds," he ended, a bit despondently, clearly still shaken by the moment.

"Damn, man. I'm sorry to hear that. What did you do then?" Jacob asked, now more engaged in this conversation than annoyed that he was no longer secluded.

"Well, thankfully my parents always harped on me to get my degree. That spring I graduated with my degree, in business management, and left college and entered the workforce. For the first five years, I felt as if I had to do everything I could to remake that million dollars. I felt it had been taken from me, and I was going to do everything I needed to do to earn it back. So I worked. Hard. To the bone. Eighty to ninety hours per week selling technology. I did pretty well but found myself stuck, kind of like you, Jake." Jacob didn't even flinch at the nickname this time.

"I got to the point one Friday night when my friends were all inviting me out for drinks, and I wouldn't go because I had too much to do. I sat at my desk and just wondered, 'Is this how I want the rest of my life to go?' I knew that it wasn't, and knew that I had to make a change," he finished.

"Wow, that's heavy. So what change did you make?" Jacob asked, very curiously.

"Well, I took the next three months and saved as much money as I could. I always wanted to be in the sports memorabilia industry. I felt like I had a great knowledge of the product. Obviously, I could sell things, and with my degree, I felt starting my own company was the way to go. So, I saved my money, took a very small investment from a friend and started Paige's Collectibles, specializing in baseball cards and rare jerseys. To this day, it is the happiest I have ever been. Even happier than the day I signed with Michigan State or ran out of that tunnel for the first time. I knew that wouldn't last. All athletic careers come to an end eventually. Mine came earlier than I expected but had it not come that early, I wouldn't be where I am today. Everything happens for a reason in this life. There are no coincidences. Even meeting you today Jacob, that isn't by chance. Anyway, gotta run. Here's my card. Stop by sometime if you wanna check out some of the awesome stuff I have."

"Thanks, Michael. No coincidences, huh? I guess not. Have a great day. Thanks for chatting with me." Jacob meant that last part now, wholeheartedly.

As Michael rose to leave, Jacob flopped back into his chair, placed his head on the narrow backing of the leather and thought, *Am I really doing something that I love? Is my brokerage my collectibles shop*? He pulled out his cell phone and dialed the only person, he thought, who would be able to answer that: Dr. Marc.

Chapter 7: Trust Your Gut

Wisdom is knowing the right path to take. Integrity is taking it.
- Unknown

This was a matter that could not wait. The news he was catching up on could wait, but talking to Dr. Marc could not. He dialed the number, his impatience growing from the first ring.

"Hello?" Dr. Marc answered.

"Dr. Marc, thanks for answering on a Saturday. I know we don't meet for another week or so, but I need to talk to you," fumbled an apologetic Jacob, determined to seek out his answer.

"Jacob, it's no problem," Dr. Marc began. "I told you to call me when you needed me, and here we are. I have nothing going on this weekend anyway, so I'm thankful you gave me something to do!"

"Thank you. That means a lot. Okay, so this morning got off to a rough start. No coffee filters this morning, couldn't even sleep as late as I wanted to. So I came to Starbucks to catch up on the news and just relax a bit, when I met a guy, completely randomly, named Michael. To be honest, I was a bit annoyed when he first came, sat down and started talking to me..."

"Jacob, let me stop you for a second, and give you this piece of advice," Dr. Marc interrupted. "First, nothing happens by chance in this life. When we have an encounter like the one you're about to tell me about, it happens for a reason. There are moments in life that you either learn from, or you let pass by. If you let them pass, it is always tough to recover those lessons. Never be so concerned with your own reality that you miss the lessons being taught. Second, well…we'll get to that. Go on."

"That makes sense. I get what you're saying. And, I'm glad that I met Michael. He's the reason why I am calling you. He talked about his football career and how that spurred him on to a job that was consuming his life. I sympathized with him when he was talking about trying to make up for the money he lost because of his injury. The thing that got me, though, was his disposition. He was positive. And, I assume that came from what he said next. He said that he eventually got to the point where he wasn't satisfied—which sounded really familiar—and decided to change things in his life. That meant starting his own business that he was passionate about, that he loved deeply. It's a sports memorabilia company. This got me thinking, 'Do I *really* love what I do?' and so I had to immediately call you when he left. Do you think this job I'm working is right for me? When we talk, does it sound like it is a passion of mine? Sorry, I know this is a bit scattered and a lot all at once ..." Jacob trailed off.

"Jacob, slow down just a little bit. Over the last few weeks that we have been in contact, you have had a lot of things thrown your way. Many different strategies and information are surely floating through your head right now, spinning with no real direction. Of all the advice that you have been given and the strategies that are being handed down, what I'm about to tell you has to be placed above all else. Even above what I just told you earlier. Is that clear?"

"Yes. I promise," Jacob confirmed.

"Okay. Good. Here it is: I can't answer that for you. Jacob, you don't want me to answer that for you."

"But, that's why I called, Dr. Marc. I've been spinning my wheels for the last two years. It feels like I've been wandering around a desert with no oasis in sight. Situations that seemed to create promise were mere mirages," Jacob interrupted.

"Jacob, stop. Take a breath for a second. I know what's going on. I know you want to succeed, but along with that success comes fulfillment. You will not have success unless you are fulfilled in gaining that success. I've been there. I get it. But no one can answer whether you are in the right line of work except you. That's it. The key piece of advice that I will give you, that you have to sear into your heart, mind, and soul is this: trust your gut."

"My gut?" Jacob asked, expecting something more for profound advice from the man he had recently come to know and trust with all he had.

"Your gut, Jacob. That pit in your stomach that will dig deeper and deeper into your soul when you are facing a decision. What is your gut telling you right now about this life-changing epiphany? That is what you need to stew on for the next day or so, Jacob. Think on your gut. What is it telling you? Once you have learned to trust that instinct and follow what your gut is telling you, you'll be able to find your purpose, which will bring you one step closer to your fulfillment. I'll talk to you later. Good talking to you, buddy," Dr. Marc said peacefully before hanging up the phone.

Chapter 8: Unique Superpower

Don't let what you cannot do interfere with what you can do.
- *John R. Wooden*

"Hey, Jakey!" Aria answered her phone, jumping at the chance to goad Jacob as often as she could.

"Aria, seriously?" he responded, unamused.

"Ah, man, lighten up a little bit. You know I kid. What's going on?"

"Well, yesterday was a full day, and by that I mean I went to Starbucks and sat down to read the news." For the next few minutes, he recounted his time with Michael Paige, and his call to Dr. Marc.

"Aria, I've thought about this over the last day and a half, and then I knew I had to call you first. I was really questioning if this work was my passion and if I could find enjoyment in it, and here's what my gut—that's Dr. Marc's advice—what my gut told me: this is my passion! I realized that the feeling I was having of wandering around a desert with no hope of relief was seated deeply inside my soul because I cared so much. I do love what I do, and I am happy that I'm in this line of work, but now I have to find out what is getting in the way of what I truly want out of this."

"Jacob! That is great to hear! I'm glad that you have gotten that out of the way. I remember being in your shoes, sitting there staring blankly into the desk calendar, watching all the squares seemingly meld into one giant block. Realizing your passion helps to remove that block. Now, I'm sure that Dr. Marc didn't say this because I'm sure he didn't want you to look anywhere except where your passion lies, but since that is established, let me ask you the question he asked me when I got to the point you are at. Okay? Ready?"

"That'd be great," confirmed Jacob.

"What's the one thing you do with TBM that really is what your company is all about?" asked Aria.

"What?" questioned Jacob.

"You heard me," she said quickly, forcing Jacob to answer immediately, "answer my question."

"Aria, you've been there from the beginning. You know exactly what I do," he pointed out. He was starting to get frustrated with her.

"That very well may be, but I want to hear you say it. Things change over the years, and I want to see if you're still on track."

"My company brokers Triple Net, or NNN, investment deals throughout the country. That was a stupid question," he said, now starting to regret that he had called to share his good news.

"Fantastic. You haven't sold out!" she said, sarcastic as ever. "Now, since that is out of the way, what is TBM's purpose? Why do you have the business?" she continued.

"What?"

"Your purpose. What is the purpose of TBM?" she continued, confident as she had ever been. "Once you start to trust your gut, just like Dr. Marc said, you'll begin to understand your purpose. What is your purpose, Jacob?"

Jacob was taken back by the fact that he had heard the exact sentence from Dr. Marc less than twenty-four hours prior. *Must be something to it*, he thought.

"Well, I started TBM back when I did to give people a different platform to sell real estate. A platform that is more cutting edge and less hassle that will generate my clients more money and stronger buyers—essentially, a better mousetrap."

"Great," she said. "Now, and I realize this is like an interrogation, but bear with me. What is the one thing that you are good at? What is your superpower, Jacob?"

"Damn, this is an interrogation! Here, I just wanted to share some good news, and you're drilling me with questions."

"If you don't want my help, I can hang up right –"

"Aria, relax. Doesn't feel as good when someone else is shooting you down, huh?" he now said sarcastically. "I appreciate all the help that you have given me. Really, I do." He truly was grateful for her guidance.

"Good. You better be." He could hear her smile through the phone. "Now, answer my question please: what is your superpower?"

"Well, if I had to answer honestly, I'd say it is my ability to build relationships and find clients," he replied after a moment.

"That's two!"

"I know it is, but honestly, they are more like a 1(a) and 1(b)." He and Aria both shared a laugh as the conversation continued. "I love meeting new people, except for yesterday when I wanted to be by myself and was promptly interrupted by Michael."

"I know, Jacob, you have always been that type of outgoing, nice-to-meet-you kind of person. What you have to do, and I will leave you with this, is to push all of your energy into those strengths. They truly are strengths. I'm not the type of people person that you are. Build those strengths."

Then she told Jacob she had to run and hung up the phone. Jacob pressed "end" on his phone, and set it down in exchange for his laptop.

* * * *

Firing up his Mac, Jacob turned on the television, just for background noise. When it was done booting up, he fired out an email to his team:

Hey guys,

I hope each and every one of you has had a wonderful weekend. Something just came to mind, and we need to meet. I would like to see every department head tomorrow morning at 8:00 a.m., in the conference room. Expect a lengthy meeting. Sorry if this conflicts with any prior engagements, but this takes priority. See you tomorrow.

Jacob

With that, Jacob began to plan out his meeting. Even on a Sunday night, the work never stopped. In the back of his mind, he was hoping his employees were taking the same initiative that he was on these off-hour nights. It was something he did expect and even had made mention of in the past. Once the agenda was set, he turned on *SportsCenter*, popped open a Coors Light and began to unwind. Tomorrow, he would hit the ground running again.

Chapter 9: Looking in the Mirror

I've learned that people will forget what you said, people will forget what you did, but people will never forget how you made them feel.
- Maya Angelou

As the night turned to morning, Jacob calmly rolled out of bed after a good night's sleep. He had spent last evening thinking about how he could convey this new revelation to his employees and had sent them a note demanding that they were at an 8:00 a.m. meeting in the conference room. He didn't think twice about their reaction to the email, because what was going be covered was of utmost importance to the brokerage firm.

He took a quick shower, put on his blue pinstriped three-piece suit, checked the notes he had made on his iPad the night before, and was out the door by 6:45 a.m., grabbing his coffee on the way.

He was at the office by 7:00, and quickly put on a pot of coffee for the team before sitting down at his desk. He again went over the notes he had made, caught up on the *New York Times Monday Briefing*, and started noticing a couple of people filing in by 7:30.

Glad to see they care, he thought, as he finished reading the last section on the current state of affairs. By 7:45, he was at his seat at the head of the table. To his right was Jamie from marketing, Jacki from administration, and—yep, Doug from sales was late. *Where the hell is he?* he quietly whispered to himself. By 8:05 everyone was in place.

"Doug, 8 a.m. too early for you?"

"Sorry, boss," Doug responded indifferently, "traffic was pretty tight on the way here."

"Hmm … maybe we could've planned for that? You know what I live by: 'to be early is to be on time, to be on time is to be too late.' At least we can get started now."

* * * *

When Jacob first started TBM, he tackled the endeavor with gusto. He recruited the best people, based on their resumes and references. He had chosen Doug, one of the top business graduates from Eastern Michigan University, straight from college, and was overwhelmed with the possibilities of what could become of his new adventure.

Through the years, he kept pushing on into the abyss, taking no prisoners and leaving those who could not keep up in the dust. There was a ton of turnover in his first couple of years because people weren't on board with his enthusiasm or vision. He did not particularly like letting people go, but he felt that if they weren't pulling their weight, then they were dead weight and needed to be cut off. After all, it was his business, and they were working for him. He always prided himself on being the first one to arrive in the morning and the last one to leave, even if that meant he was getting to the bars a little later on Friday nights and the talent was a little picked through. He ultimately would get what he wanted by night's end.

In the first few years, there was no relationship that he counted on with his employees: they were "just employees," after all. He ran TBM exactly how he had envisioned when he used to sit in his office at WSR, and he was making money, closing deals and, to a point, felt successful.

Then, in year four, it all came to a screeching halt. No longer did he enjoy what he was doing. Now, he was stuck, sitting at his desk late at night, getting nothing done. Was it his employees? Was this what he wanted from his life? These were all questions that engulfed his mind, day in and day out in his fourth year. And, for the last three weeks, he had been on a journey of discovery, starting that one night with Aria at Cafe D'Mongo's.

* * * *

"Now that we are all here, let's begin," Jacob commanded. He was ruling the meeting the way he ran the business, with a stern and expectant voice. "I know that we usually meet on Tuesday mornings, and we will still meet tomorrow, but over the weekend I had an epiphany pertaining to TBM, and it had to be shared and discussed right now." Eyes were not rolling, but everyone in the room could feel the tension.

It wasn't that the employees disliked Jacob. They generally did like him. He had hired them and made each of them heads of their respective divisions. But, there was just something about being there that put each of them on the edge of their seats.

"Now, you all know that *I* started this company four years ago in the hopes of setting a better mousetrap for clients in the NNN deals. Again, this weekend I realized how much I love what *I* do here. Through various conversations, I also came to realize that maybe *we* have been dropping the ball lately. The clients are not rolling in like they used to. Without clients, of course, we have nothing. So, here's the deal: by the end of the day today, I want each of you to construct a list of potential clients that we can go after, plus one 'white whale,'" he said, very confident in this directive.

"Jacob–" Doug shot in, "not all of us deal with clients." He was right, but Jacob wasn't having it and cut him off before he could finish his thought.

"Doug!" he said, "You're right, but today, you do. Listen, *my* greatest strengths lie in my ability to build relationships with clients, and if I have no clients to build relationships with, well then, what are we really doing around here?" he queried.

For the rest of the morning, Jacob discussed his new tactic and how they could each get their job done to his liking. He went after the discussion with the vim and vigor of a bull going after a matador's red cape. He was charging hell with a squirt gun, and they either jumped on the bandwagon or got out of the way. At lunchtime, he released them to their tasks and headed out for a quick bite.

Refreshed, he returned to put his own nose to the grindstone. By the end of the day, he had three new clients on his desk, no white whales. It was 7:00 in the evening, and the rest of his employees had gone home an hour ago.

What the hell is this? Was I not clear enough? He asked himself, his unfulfilled spirit turning bitter. As he began to pack up his things for the night, he took a quick glance at his desk calendar. Penciled in for tomorrow evening was a scheduled meeting with Dr. Marc, the first of their monthly meetings.

Good, he thought, at least we'll have something to talk about tomorrow. He turned off his computer monitor, grabbed his bag, and headed toward the parking lot. He had gotten no farther ahead than he was when he left on Friday, and certainly nowhere close to where he had imagined he'd be after his Sunday night planning session.

"Maybe this is it. Maybe this is all there is to this company," he said out loud, to no one in particular.

Chapter 10: Unintentional Chaos and Serendipity

Change before you have to.
- Jack Welch

As Jacob pulled out of his parking space, he sat in silence. Normally his drives were full of noise from the podcasts, books on tape, or local sports talk show as he would drive and listen and often argue with the opinions of the hosts, even though they never could hear his well-made points. But he didn't argue tonight. He was frustrated with his employees' lack of participation and his own feeling of being trapped on the proverbial hamster wheel professionally. Tonight, he made sure that he had his lucky golf ball with him. With his left hand firmly gripping the steering wheel in the twelve o'clock position, he twirled his precious little pearl between his fingers. This helped to settle him.

As he entered his apartment, he set his bag against the leg of the kitchen table before finding half of a leftover hamburger from Saturday in the fridge. He ate his measly dinner then reached for the bourbon and poured a heftier portion than he normally did. He dropped into his favorite leather chair, grabbed his laptop again and emailed his team.

Guys,

Today's meeting was necessary, but the results were minimal. For tomorrow's meeting, I need you to think about the following points and come ready to contribute. This will be in addition to the weekly updates from each of your departments, as well as the additional information that will be on the agenda tomorrow. Here's what I want you to think about:

1.) What or how can you work to bring in new leads and clients?

2.) How do we differentiate ourselves from our competition and how are we communicating that message?

3.) What is the action plan to make everything happen?

This last one is major. Probably the biggest question that I need to be answered. We have to do things differently to extend our reach and offer our services to people who don't yet know they need it. In order to do this, we need all hands on deck.

Have a good night. See you at 8:00 a.m. Don't be late! Jacob

He closed the computer and took a swig from his snifter. The warming burn of the rich, brown liquor helped relax him more. Now, he sat—satisfied—with his left hand draped around the glass, resting it on the leather armrest and succumbing to the bouncing blue lights reflecting from the television.

* * * *

As the night gave way to morning, Jacob rolled over in bed, refreshed and ready to attack the day. As he went through his morning routine, his mind began to slip back towards yesterday's shortfalls. His adrenaline started to rise, and the aggravation he felt as he left the office the night before began to creep back in. He quickly reminded himself that today was a new day, and then made his way towards the office.

Again, he arrived before everyone else. But, this was the norm. By 7:45 he was in his chair at the head of the conference table, his agenda placed before him, and his tablet standing at attention just off to his right, so he had a good view of the screen. Jacki was the first to arrive, and he greeted her. She looked tired and returned Jacob's greeting with just a small nod of the head.

Soon after, Doug from sales walked in, and he looked flustered.

"Everything okay?" Jacob asked.

"Yeah, I'm fine." Doug said, not giving Jacob the opportunity for a follow-up. The abruptness caught Jacob off guard, and he gave a little concerned look in Doug's direction.

"It's nothing," replied Doug to the gaze, "rough morning."

"You're good now, though, for the meeting?" The response came off a lot worse than Jacob had intended it. Nonetheless, once the words were spoken, there was not much to be done.

"I'll be fine," was the response as Doug left a seat between himself and Jacki, moving himself further down the table from Jacob.

There's a statement! Jacob thought to himself as he noticed the empty chair immediately to his right. As the clock turned to 8:00 a.m., Jamie hurriedly came through the door and threw herself into the seat next to Jacob.

As the meeting progressed, each person reported on his or her respective departments. Each report was detailed and positive. And, each of them had gotten Jacob's email the night before and gave their answers to his questions. Each had good ideas on reaching new clients, and each said they were in for the goal and mission of Jacob's company.

This pleased Jacob, but he continued to wonder, *why, then, are we just spinning the wheels? What more can we do to grow this business?* These were questions he had been mulling over long before that night at Cafe D'Mongo's with Aria. And the answers seemed to slip further away with each passing day. Luckily, or unluckily, he was meeting with Dr. Marc tonight for dinner. This allowed Jacob to breathe a sigh of relief as he looked toward the future of his business.

* * * *

Dr. Marc had called Jacob earlier in the day to say he would meet him at TBM. They would ride together to the restaurant. Also, Dr. Marc wanted to check things out at TBM. Jacob agreed and continued on with his day until his visitor arrived. Jacob quickly jumped up from his desk, adjusted the tie that was normally loosened during the workday, and met Dr. Marc at his office door.

"Good afternoon, sir," Jacob said.

"Sir? Jacob, call me Marc. My father goes by 'sir,'" he smiled as he said it, calming Jacob's nerves a little bit. "How's it going around here?"

"It's going..." Jacob responded, a bit of despondency in his voice.

"Jacob, it's a process. Things you want to succeed at need time. They do not happen overnight." As he was finishing his little coaching session, Jacki walked in with a stack of papers, frazzled, and barely able to open the door. Dr. Marc hopped from where he was, grabbing the door handle to assist her. The agility surprised Jacob.

"Jacob, here ya go, here's the list of new client contacts I've been generating, and the projections you wanted from the administration. It's 6:30. I'm going to head home if that's okay?"

"It is, Jacki. Have a good night!" Jacob said with an excitement she hadn't heard before. She did a double take, and it did not go unnoticed by Dr. Marc.

"Hey, Jacob, can we reschedule this dinner meeting for tomorrow night?" Dr. Marc asked.

"Um, everything okay?" Jacob said, now worried that Jacki's presence had dissuaded the dentist from their meeting, which he would come to find out was true.

"Yeah, things are fine, I still want to meet, but I want to meet somewhere closer to my office. Come by tomorrow around 3:30. We'll meet at my office, and then go to dinner and talk business. Sound good? Plus, I'll buy." Dr. Marc smiled, pouring as much sarcasm as he could muster onto that last statement.

"Sure," Jacob replied, now worried. "I'll come by, and we can push the meeting." With an almost defeated tone, Jacob shook Dr. Marc's hand and showed him out.

Jacob sat down at his desk, defeated by the fact that he had been looking forward to this meeting with Dr. Marc, and now he was relegated to more of a less-than-desirable dinner; yet, he found the prospects of finding a local bar, eating there, drinking, and mingling with whatever female may come his way was an acceptable alternative to make up for the lost night. He tossed his lucky Titleist up and down a couple of times, turned off the monitor, and closed down the building.

* * * *

Jacob pulled into the parking spot at Oak Tree Tavern, a small local bar that he had been to before. This was his place of solitude, especially after a long day's work. He could come in here, listen to some live blues and enjoy a nice hamburger with sweet potato fries. In his opinion, it was the best unknown spot in the city. And, it was not that far from work. Sometimes, he would come here for lunch when he could sneak away from the office, but most of the time it was on Friday nights.

The musicians were, as usual, located to the left of the patrons as they entered the door. Tonight, on a Tuesday, a solo artist with an acoustic guitar was performing. It was the exact type of music Jacob needed to hear to relax. Jacob took his seat to the right of the door, in his favorite corner booth.

"Hey, Jake!" called the bubbly waitress named Ruth. Secretly she had a crush on the young businessman. Jacob knew it, and he played along.

"Hey there, Ruth," he said. "What's new?"

"Well, not a lot. School started back up, and I got into the College of Education at Wayne State," she responded. Jacob was reminded why he never went after Ruth. She was too young. There were limits to these sort of things; although he did wonder.

"That's great," he congratulated her, still enjoying the game they played. "I'm sure you will make a great teacher. Say, how's Jimmy doing?" he asked, inquiring about the owner of the Tavern.

"He's great. Things around here have been going really well. Been busy every weekend. He'll be glad when I tell him you stopped by. We all really like seeing you around here," she said, now pouring it on. "How have you been, Jacob?"

"I've been better. Work's overtaking my mind a lot lately, but we don't need to talk about that. In fact, I'd prefer not to. Would you please get me a bour –"

"Bourbon on the rocks, two green olives. Got ya. I'll be right back." She almost kicked herself for not bringing it to him as soon as she saw him walk through the door. That would've impressed him for sure.

As he waited for his drink, Jacob sat back in the booth, scrolling through his phone and looking at nothing in particular. The guy with the guitar had begun to play only instrumentals. As Jacob peered over the edge of his smartphone, he noticed the bar's newest patron.

In through the door walked a woman, medium height and a slender build. She had dirty blonde hair about shoulder length that she pulled into a messy ponytail the moment she found herself a seat. She sat with her back to Jacob, at a table for one. From the moment that Jacob saw her walk in, he knew he had to meet her. His focus was quickly cut off by the bubbly waitress, "Here ya go, Jacob! Hope you like it," Ruth said.

"Thanks," he said, not even looking up to meet her eye. "Say, Ruth? Have you ever seen that woman in here?" he asked, not necessarily caring how it looked to her. He had one priority and concern in this instance, and that was to find out who that girl was. "She been in here before? I know I've never seen her."

"Maybe once or twice," said Ruth in a disappointed but hopeful tone. "Say, Jake, why don't I find out what she's drinking and play matchmaker for ya. I know you probably need all the help you can get anyway." She forced that one, and the delivery was off, but the offer was genuine. She knew he was older, and that was all right. Maybe if they remained friends, someday something could happen. Plus, she was busy with school now anyway, at least that's what she kept telling herself.

"Yeah, Ruth. Do that."

"Done," she smiled at him.

After a few minutes, Jacob watched as Ruth took a crisp glass of white sauvignon blanc to the woman's table. Ruth's smile was as natural as ever. She was definitely a pro. She pointed back towards Jacob. The woman turned, and Jacob gave one of those forced and awkward waves. The lady tipped her glass to Jacob, and he waved her over.

Both smiled, and in a moment, she was seated across from him.

"Thanks for the drink," she said. It was not the first time she had received a drink from a stranger, but tonight she didn't care for some reason. As she sat down across the booth from Jacob, she soon realized how easy it was to have a conversation with him.

"I'm Jacob," he began. "Sorry if that was a typical move, but at least you're sitting across from me now."

"It was a bit obvious, and it has been done before, but I don't mind the company tonight," she said, not concerned with speaking her mind.

"Good. I could use the company, too," he responded. "Your name?"

"Oh, I guess I forgot that part," she said, blushing at the obvious gaffe. Jacob noticed the slight smirk that she gave at that moment and instantly he was swept up in her charming presence. "I'm Joanna Leigh. Sorry about that."

"Beautiful name," noted Jacob. He was succinct but unmeasured. He had spoken to women plenty of times, and she was definitely not the first girl for whom he had bought a drink, but he found himself in new territory as he watched her swirl the golden liquid around her glass while looking at him. "What do you do, Joanna Leigh?"

"Well, I have my degree in nursing from the University of Michigan. I work most nights at the Children's Hospital, but tonight I'm enjoying a night off. So, here I am, sitting with you and enjoying this wonderful glass of wine. What about you, Jacob, or do you go by Jake?"

"Jacob. My mother used to call me Jakey, and I hated that, so I prefer Jacob. I own my real estate brokerage firm, TBM. We are nationwide. It's right down the block."

"So you're here often?" Joanna asked.

"Well, I'm not a bar rat who drowns his nights in a tavern then hopes to make it home, if that's what you're asking." This was his best attempt in the initial meeting at flirting. He was actually nervous.

"That is not what I meant at all," she responded quickly so as not to give the wrong impression. "I'm sorry if that came out wrong."

"No, no. I'm just giving you a hard time," Jacob saved himself. As they talked about their different careers, the minutes turned to hours. Before they knew it, midnight was approaching. Each had ordered a couple more drinks while they talked, and normally at this point Jacob would be looking to close the deal. But, not tonight. Something inside of him nudged him to just ask for Joanna's number. So, he took a shot.

"Say, it's getting late. Do you think we could continue this conversation some other time?" It was a calculated question. Her body language throughout the night had encouraged him. Her hair went from pulled back and unapproachable to down and less reserved. He didn't know exactly when that transition happened, but he was definitely aware of it.

"I would like that," she said with a smile. Jacob smiled back. She wrote her number on a small napkin and handed it across the table. Jacob carefully folded it and placed it in his right breast pocket. He motioned for Ruth to bring the check, and explained that tonight was on him. Their first unofficial date—of course, that was a thought he only kept in his head, hoping not to jinx something wonderful.

As they exited the bar, Jacob flagged down a cab for Joanna Leigh, told her he would call her in the next few days, and opened the car door for her. He didn't swoop in for anything—no kiss, no hug, not even an awkward handshake—he just let her go. He tapped on the back of the cab signaling that it was good to go, and watched as the taillights disappeared down the road. He got into his car and headed home. Smiling the entire way.

Too bad I couldn't have dinner with Dr. Marc, he thought with a smile. Yeah, too bad.

Chapter 11: Necessary Feedback

Intelligence is the ability to adapt to change.
- Stephen Hawkins

Jacob went through the next day with a bit of a distraction. Not only had he just met Joanna (and couldn't get her off his mind), but also today he would be meeting with Dr. Marc. Only Joanna had been able to take his mind off of this event.

Yesterday had been strange. Dr. Marc was in Jacob's office ready to go, and then all of a sudden something came up. *Jacki probably scared him off*, he thought. It definitely was not anything he had done.

He went through his afternoon trying to turn his attention to the business. The day passed, and he accomplished nothing. Once again, he was stuck with no direction and no answers. His meeting with Dr. Marc was needed now more than ever.

As he sat alone in his office, the light from the computer screen masked his face while he sighed heavily, tossing his lucky Titleist. Up and down, and up and down went the ball, with no direction other than the one that Jacob gave it. *Just like TBM*, he thought. *Just like TBM.*

On the last toss, Jacob mishandled the small orb and it fumbled onto his desk. He watched it roll across his desk calendar, passing right over the date one week from today: his company's anniversary. This would be his fifth year at the helm of TBM Brokerage, and by far this had been his most difficult.

What do I have to celebrate next week? he whispered to himself. *This year has been terrible, except for last night, of course; but there has been no growth, no new ideas, my employees seem to have given up. What is there to celebrate?*

As the words came to his mind, he grabbed a pale yellow Post-It note from his desk drawer and clicked his ballpoint pen. In big block letters, he wrote: "Why celebrate?" Then, he mindlessly colored in the letters. *Why celebrate?* He wondered. *Damn, if that isn't the saddest thing...* he said to no one at all.

I can't believe this is the point that we have reached. Something. Must. Change.

* * * *

As the 3:30 appointment time drew close, Jacob packed his bag and headed toward Dr. Marc's office. He arrived promptly at 3:25, always ensuring that he was comfortably on time for everything. As he drove to the office, he kept thinking about the words he had just scribbled on the Post-It.

Why celebrate?

It was a question that in its mere twenty-minute existence haunted him deeply. The moment he had placed ink to paper, a charcoal cloud enveloped him, drowning out the colors of his surroundings, erasing them into non-existence. Now there was only the bleakness of a black and white existence.

He parked his car in the visitor lot and sat for a few minutes as the car idled. He let the coolness of the air conditioning brush against his face. He breathed deeply to collect himself before heading in. Of course, he could not let Dr. Marc see him in this bewildered state, even though he knew that he wouldn't be able to pull one over on him either.

What struck Jacob as he sat in the car was the understated nature of the building that housed Dr. Marc's practice. It was a small, single-story, red brick that cheerfully welcomed its visitors with a full wall of windows revealing the goings-on inside. The lawn around the building was neatly trimmed, even though it did seem like it was close to needing a cut soon. Next to the walkway leading to the front door was a sign that read, "MLD Dental: We'll make you proud of your smile."

Jacob pulled open the front door and was greeted by a middle-aged woman, slender and blonde, in typical dental office scrubs. She was bright and bubbly – the type of person who can go overboard on the cheeriness. Jacob was not in the mood for one of those types, but as the guest, he could do nothing but smile.

"Good afternoon, sir. How may I help you?" she said in a fast, high-pitched voice. Jacob thought, *am I the first person she had seen all day? No, definitely not.* But she was certainly excited to see him even though they had never met. This took Jacob by surprise and made him notice that all the employees had a certain energy about them.

Jacob was not big on energy. He had been around people who were firm believers in energy and its ability to affect you personally. Those with positive energy were more productive and overall had a more pleasant disposition towards everyday life. Yet, those on the other end of the spectrum with negative energy were the extreme opposite. They were much more pessimistic and less productive. Jacob had never bought into this ideology. In fact, sometimes when he heard people speak about their energy he rolled his eyes. Well, not always physically but at least mentally.

As he waited patiently for Dr. Marc, Jacob set himself in a corner where he could simply observe the office. He made a concerted effort to ignore his phone, placing it on vibrate, and just watched how the office worked. What struck him was this energy. It was the only word that kept coming to mind. Energy. Every person in the dentist's office was happy to be there. Every employee conducted himself or herself in much the same way as the assistant who greeted Jacob. All were congenial, overflowing with personality, and made every single person there feel important. And, the biggest thing Jacob noticed through his observation was that the positive energy was contagious. Even the patrons seemed happy to be there. Who's happy to go to the dentist? Jacob noticed it tugging at his own demeanor as well, and he began to smile at the thought of it.

* * * *

After about an hour, Dr. Marc came to the front of the office and greeted Jacob with a firm handshake and a smile. Having been caught up in his observation of the office, Jacob had not even noticed the hour that had passed. Even if he had, there was no way Jacob would've been upset with the dentist.

"Hi there, Jacob. Good to see you," said Dr. Marc as he greeted him.

"Sir, how are you doing?"

"I thought we talked about that 'sir' thing. Just call me Marc or Dr. Marc," the dentist chided his mentee. "Thanks again for rescheduling. You know, there was a reason for it."

"Everything okay?" asked Jacob.

"For me, yes. But yesterday when I came by, I'll be honest, I was a bit irritated when I saw your office," Dr. Marc said in a stern fashion that made it clear he was not pleased. And with this, a pit started to grow in Jacob's stomach.

"Was it Jacki?" Jacob asked, concerned that his worst fears were coming true.

"Who? The lady who frantically came in and out of your office? No. She's not the problem Jacob."

"No?" Jacob asked, the pit growing larger and larger. He was pretty sure it was about to overtake his midsection.

"No," was the abrupt answer. "She wasn't. But I can tell you what is."

"Please do," Jacob said, more curious and worried than he'd been in recent memory.

"Frankly, the problem, Jacob, is you." The pit now was in Jacob's throat, and he felt like he was swallowing a balloon. Instantly his mouth went dry, and his face became hot. He was not happy with this revelation.

"Me? What in the world do you mean? How could I possibly be the problem?" For a moment he had forgotten that they were still standing in the waiting area of the office, and there were other patients around. The world had not stopped turning, but people inside were starting to notice the two men having a conversation. "That can't be right," Jacob finally said, irritated.

"Jacob, come into my office. No need to have this conversation out here."

"Sorry. Lead the way." As they headed back to Marc's office, all Jacob could think was, *how the hell am I the problem? That place doesn't exist without me!*

"Jacob, please, sit. Let me explain myself."

"I wish you would. Doc, I'm very thankful that you have taken me under your wing, but I have to disagree with you on this one," Jacob sputtered.

"I'm going to stop you there. I decided to help you, and that means that I'm going to help you. Even if what I have to say to you isn't something that you necessarily want to hear. Most of the time when we can't figure out what the problem is, it is because we have failed to look at the main culprit: ourselves. And this is exactly where you are at." Dr. Marc took a sip from the white ceramic coffee cup he was holding. "Can I get you something to drink?"

"Do you have anything stronger than coffee?" came the sarcastic reply.

"No, son. I gave that up a long time ago."

"I'll be fine. What do you mean that I am the problem?" Jacob prodded.

"It's quite simple, Jacob. You are the person who sets the tone for your organization. And those under you follow your example. Ninety-five percent of the things you do, say, and even *think* set the tone for the culture of your company. Yesterday I was in there and saw that poor young lady frazzled and completely drowned in her work. It spoke volumes. It told me all I needed to know about your leadership style. It starts with you, Jacob, *you* are the fountainhead from which springs either positive or negative energy. Especially in your company."

There it was again, that talk of energy. Jacob immediately felt the twinge of discomfort flood his soul.

"You were there for all of ten minutes, how could you poss—" Dr. Marc cut him off.

"Ten minutes was all I needed, Jacob. It's really quite simple. Do you know why I left you waiting for over an hour today?" Dr. Marc sat back in his chair and looked in Jacob's direction. "I was hoping you would take the time to observe my office. Now, admittedly, I'm not perfect, nor would I ever tell you that I have it all figured out. But forty years in this business and having grown it past the point of worrying about it failing has given me a leg to stand on. So right here and now I'll leave you with a choice. You can either sit, swallow your pride—which is probably what got you to this point—and listen, or we can shake hands, and I can wish you the best of luck. Which will it be?"

Damn! Jacob thought, as he stared past Dr. Marc and focused on the dental degree hanging behind his desk. What seemed to take three days, really only lasted about thirty seconds. Finally, Jacob mustered the courage to speak.

"Doc, I really do want your help. I need your help. Problem is, I've never truly had help before. I don't know where to begin. I sure as hell don't know how to hear the type of words you just spoke to me. That was brutal."

"I won't apologize for them. Jacob, too often we feel as though if we work harder, stay busier, and expect the impossible from ourselves and everyone associated with us then we can rule the world. But, too often, all we do is alienate those people and run ourselves into an early grave. I know at your age, you think you're invincible, indestructible, and know everything. That's not to cut you down—maybe a little—but it's to tell you that I've been there. I understand it. I'm dead serious, though, you have a choice to make: you either want the help I'm willing to give, or you can keep clenching your fists, driving your people farther and farther down, and eventually lose your business. It's up to you. I cannot make that determination for you. It has to come from deep within your soul. If you do not believe it and accept it there first, then you'll never trust me enough or be willing to accept help."

Though the sun was setting and day was giving way to evening, the room appeared to be getting brighter. As Jacob continued to look past Dr. Marc, the room became luminous. Almost immediately after Dr. Marc finished talking, Jacob sat forward, placed his elbows onto his knees and dropped his face into his hands. He did not cry. He felt the suffocating feeling of being overwhelmed. The room began to grow brighter, but Jacob's soul grew darker.

The reality was dawning upon Jacob that Dr. Marc was absolutely right—Jacob knew that he was. He was on this journey with the destination in sight and Dr. Marc's words paved the path leading to it. But, tied around his waist was a rope pulling him further and further from where he needed to be. It was the memory of all he had done before, and all he *would need* to do soon to finally reach his destination. As he sat in the chair in Dr. Marc's office with his hands firmly supporting his face, he physically felt the tug of war taking place inside of him. As he wrestled with who he was and who he wanted to become, he thought of the one person who had always made everything all right: his mother, Wendy.

* * * *

Jacob's mother, Wendy, had passed away when he was in college. Even though she was gone physically, her presence lived on inside Jacob. With each new day he faced, he felt her calming demeanor within him, helping him to face whatever the day may bring. As he sat now in Dr. Marc's office, rubbing his temples ever so gently, he was reminded of his most fond memory of his mother. And, it was the most perfect time to experience this random flashback.

The den in his parents' home was a small, square room at the back of the house. The distinguishing feature of the den was the brick fireplace that divided the back wall. The hearth held a stack of unused firewood on the left and all the pokers and steel shovels needed for fireplace maintenance on the right. In front of the fireplace sat the most comfortable leather love seat, with a high back and fluffy pillows. It was the perfect place for a warm nap on a cold Sunday afternoon in Michigan. It was also his mother's favorite place in the house for one reason: the record player.

In the corner of the den stood a round wooden table upon which sat a Sony record player—not one of the cheap modern imitations, but the real McCoy. Every piece of vinyl that hit that turntable clicked and popped, and the sound became comforting to Jacob.

Jacob came into the den one Friday afternoon after school and found his mother sitting on the leather seat. Her favorite song—one that Jacob knew all the words to by his seventh year—was playing at just the right volume level. As he entered, he heard, "*What a world, what a life, I'm in love ... I've got the world on a string...*" It was Ol Blue Eyes, the Chairman of the Board himself: Frank Sinatra. Jacob did not want to interrupt her since she rarely had time to herself, but she already knew he was there.

"Hey, Jakey. How's it going? How was school? Oooh, tell me, how did the big election go?"

Jacob had told his parents a few weeks ago that he was planning on running for sophomore class president. They weren't surprised by this announcement but they certainly were elated that he was going to jump into such a valued position.

"You won, didn't you? Oh, don't hold back, Jakey. Tell me! I'm dying here!" she said, so excited she almost forgot to let him actually answer the question.

"Well..." Jacob started, "the election was today, but I pulled my name from the running." He tried to make the mortar shell of information he'd just spat land as softly as he could. The last thing he ever wanted to do was disappoint either of his parents, and over the last couple of weeks, they had given him some advice and tips on how to win.

"What? Jakey, baby, why?" she responded, a bit disappointed. "I thought for sure you were ready and even excited about running? No?"

"I was, and Mom, I know you guys really wanted me to run. I was just afraid to lose. I didn't feel like anyone wanted to vote for me. But, I do appreciate all you and Dad did for me, trying to help. I just wasn't ready, I guess," he said with his eyes glued to his toes, unwilling to look his mom in the eyes.

"Jacob," her voice was a bit more stern than cordial, "why would you do something like that? You were going to be such a great class president. What on earth made you decide to just jump out of the race?" She had shifted her tone now, trying not to be disappointed. She never wanted her children to think they were letting her down.

"I don't know, Mom. To be honest, I just didn't think I had it in me."

"Oh, honey. Listen, I think this is a great opportunity for you to learn something about life. Can you just sit and listen for a second, Jakey?"

"Sure," Jacob responded, not really knowing what to expect.

"Sweetie, before I say anything else I want you to know one thing," she paused as Jacob made his way to the couch and sat next to her, both of their bodies turned at an angle so they could look at each other. "Above anything else I tell you today, I want you to know that I love you more than anything in this world. Your father and I are very proud of all that you have accomplished from sports to school and even the friends that you have chosen for yourself. We are grateful that you are our little boy."

She placed a hand on the back of his neck and started to take pieces of his hair between her fingers, so as to add a sense of physical touch to the words she was saying.

"You know your father and I love you very much, and there is nothing in this world that you could possibly do to make us love you any less, nor is there anything that would make us love you more. You're our boy, but you must understand one thing: being fearful of losing is no reason for not trying. It is better in life to have tried and lost, than to have not tried at all. But, know that we love you. Do we have that straight?" She smiled, still fingering the hairs on his head.

"Yes, Mom. I know." Jacob responded with that typical teenage annoyance at the sentimentality of the moment.

"Good. Now hear me when I say, there is *nothing* in this world that you cannot do as long as you put your mind to it and give it all you've got." She paused for a moment, releasing the hair on the back of his head, and made her way to the record player. She dropped the needle at the precise groove to drive her point home.

"Listen to the first words of this song, I know that you know them, but I want you to really think about them." The record screeched and began to play, "*I've got the world on a string, I'm sitting on a rainbow, I've got that string around my fi-in-ger...*" Jacob mouthed the words as they came through the speakers.

"*... can't you see I'm in love.* It's a love song, Mom. I *know* what the song's about." That was an easy one.

"No, well, yes, son, it is a love song. But how does being in love make Sinatra *feel*?" she prodded.

"Well, it seems like he feels all mushy, all lovey dovey. The guy's got a song to sing. He can make the rain go any time he waves his finger. A bunch of mush." A typical teenage response.

"No, you're missing the point. *Love* is a feeling and state of mind that focuses around one thing: passion. So you can really say that this song is about finding something that you're passionate about. And when you do, you'll have the world on a string. For Sinatra, that was a woman, but it could be a class presidency, or maybe a career someday. Here's what you really need to see: when you have the world on a string, which means the power to accomplish anything that is inside of you, anything you want to accomplish can be accomplished when you have the passion behind it and hold the world on the end of a string."

She came back over and sat again looking at Jacob.

"Now, to get there, you're going to need help. You couldn't have done this presidency by yourself, nor will you be able to accomplish anything without the help of others. The passion comes from you. The advice and help are how others fulfill their passions. Now listen to me, Jacob, whenever in life you want to grab the world by a string and really conquer it, surround yourself with people who can help. And take their advice."

* * * *

...Whenever in life you want to grab the world by a string and really conquer it, surround yourself with people who can help. And take their advice.

The words rang in Jacob's ears. Here he was faced with a question from Dr. Marc: did Jacob want his help or not? He knew what his mother would say, and he knew that he was so close to grabbing the string that was tied around the world and that he would soon hold it tightly. He just needed a little boost to get there.

His face shot up from his hands, and his back straightened in the chair.

"I'm in. I'm the problem. I've been the problem, and now I have to fix the problem."

"That's great!" Dr. Marc sat back, pleased with whatever revelation had come Jacob's way. "First things first. You will need a business coach. Now, I know you think *I'm* the business coach, but that is not the case. There are people who actually do this for a living. I'm here to be a part of your personal board of directors and to help you with the coming transformation of your business. I've worked with business coaches, and they do help to transform the culture of companies. Something, no doubt, TBM needs. Here's his card. One thing, however, Jacob, you may think that hiring a coach is a bad thing. Some people think that. It's not. No World Series ring or Lombardi trophy was ever won without a coach. This a good thing. A very good thing for you and your business."

Jacob reached across the desk and took the small rectangle of information, and he studied the front side of it. Sam Cobb. White Hall Business Coaching.

"Thanks, Doc. I will make sure to give him a call as soon as I can. *Tomorrow*." Jacob slid the card into his pocket and shook Dr. Marc's hand. He began to feel that the imaginary rope that was constricting his waist and pulling him farther and farther from where he wanted to be, was finally—slowly—starting to loosen its grip.

Part Two:
The Business Coach

Chapter 12: The Business Coach Arrives

You don't learn to walk by following rules. You learn by doing and falling over.
- Sir Richard Branson, Virgin Group Founder

Jacob awoke the next morning at his usual time, his breath still smelling of last night's Thai dinner he shared with Dr. Marc. It was a great meeting. He got dressed, made his morning coffee, and then headed out the door to work. He was destined to get there a bit earlier than everyone else and planned to take a little detour. He stopped at a local Dunkin' Donuts, knowing that if he was going to change the culture of his business, it was not going to happen overnight. But, he could at least treat his people to a morning coffee and doughnut.

As Jacob set the doughnuts and carton of coffee on the conference room table, he positioned a handwritten note beside it.

"Team, thanks for all you do. Have one on me.
– Jacob"

Jacob sat at his desk as his employees filed in. They saw the doughnuts but seemed hesitant to touch them, as if they truly could not believe where they came from.

Eventually, Jamie jumped in, and everyone else followed suit.

Damn, I really must have these guys scared, Jacob thought.

Jacob waited until just before 10:00 in the morning to dial the number on the card he had received from Dr. Marc yesterday. He carefully set the card beside the telephone and pressed each number pad with caution. As he dialed, butterflies began to dance inside his stomach. This was not the same feeling he had the day before when he saw the anniversary of his company on his calendar. That was vastly different, nearly suffocating. This was that first date, fear of the unknown, I-hope-they-like-me nerves.

"Hello," a soft, deep, scratchy voice said on the other line, "this is Sam."

"Hel-lo, sir," Jacob said with a slightly shaky voice. He cleared his throat and continued, "Sir, hello. My name is Jacob Wengrow. A close associate of mine, Marc Gardner, gave me your business card yesterday. He's been advising me on some business matters and recommended that I speak to an actual business coach. Do you have some time to talk? Sorry to bombard you," Jacob apologetically said into the receiver.

"Hello, Jacob. Thanks for calling. I only have about fifteen minutes, but that's plenty of time for us to get to know each other and figure out if this could work or not. You mind if I ask you some questions? I do this with all potential clients. Helps give a pretty good preliminary reading," Sam said.

"Sure," came the response, "shoot."

"Well, Jacob, first, let me ask you this: what do you want to accomplish working with someone like me?"

The question was not exactly what Jacob was expecting, and so he had to ask Sam to repeat it. He did, and Jacob thought as he heard the question now for the second time.

"Well, Sam, I guess the only way to answer that question is to say that I feel stuck in the business I'm running. Well, more like the business that is running me. It's something that has been going on for about a year, but I just started to actually feel the stranglehold it had on me in the last couple of months. The business is a brokerage company that I started about four years ago, almost five now. But, lately, it has just become stale and complacent."

"Stuck, huh?" Sam replied. "Sounds like you are wishing for growth but don't see any happening. Now, you're looking for someone to get you out of being stuck *in* your business, to working *on* your business. Right?"

"Exactly."

"Well, good. That's exactly what I do. I'd be glad to take you on. I can hear the desire in your voice. First thing first, we have to get the right people in the right seats, setting them up to succeed by putting them in a position to use their unique abilities—their superpowers if you will—and that may mean cleaning up the business, cutting the excess. I won't know what that looks like until I meet with you, all of your employees, and get a feel for the culture of your company. Let's set up a time later this week—say Friday at lunch? I'll come in and conduct my interviews and set a plan for us going forward. Will that work for you?"

Jacob checked his desk calendar and noticed—just like most other days—Friday was wide open. No client meetings to speak of.

"Friday is perfect," he said excitedly into the phone. "But, let me just warn you: recently, I've been told that the culture around here isn't great—in fact that bombshell was dropped on me yesterday—no one's fault but my own. Hopefully, it's not beyond repair. I'd hate to waste your time." Jacob had not noticed, but as he said those words, his gaze dropped to the tops of his shoes, like an ashamed child who had been scolded.

"Jacob, please let's not get ahead of ourselves. I've been in some pretty sticky situations. You just have to work with me, take some advice, and *want* the change. If you can promise me that, then we can work together. Do not hold back on me. Give me all you got, and we'll get this thing on the right track. That you can take to the bank," Sam said with a confidence that brought Jacob's gaze up from his shoes and off into the distance. Then Sam continued, "Friday we'll meet, just you and I to go over your organizational chart, business plan, and then set something up for the following week and get started." He definitely liked Sam so far. Now he just had to wait to meet him in person on Friday.

* * * *

Sam Cobb was a simple man. He was a business coach in his early fifties who had got his start in real estate. The first thing anyone ever noticed about Sam was his appearance. Not because it was a bad sight, but because it was a good one. He stood six feet tall and had a full head of black hair flecked with gray that was neatly cut into a nice right-to-left combover. He possessed a Thor-like jawline that was cleanly shaved every day by the straight edge of a barber. He always dressed impeccably.

He was a creature of habit, waking up early every morning to play basketball, tennis, or swim at the local recreation center. Thus, he was in excellent shape. His favorite time of the week was his weekly bridge game, usually played in his own backyard. He always met his three closest friends for the game, one of whom was Billy Franklin, the business partner who helped Sam build a successful business.

For twenty-five years, Sam bought, sold, and negotiated residential home developments. He liked the idea of being in the business of building and constructing homes and subdivisions, but was not a skilled builder. He knew his strengths and found someone in Billy Franklin—his bridge partner—who was a terrific builder in need of a sales guy. Sam became the face of the company, while Bill became the hands.

Their office was located just off Main Street in Milford, Michigan. That location gave them a wonderful view of the runoff from Hubble Pond, a serene setting for all of their business dealings. Sam was the rainmaker who negotiated prices for land and construction, dealing primarily with the eager new homebuyers. He would oversee the process of the residential development, and he was good at what he did. Bill was, too, which is why they worked so well together.

Sam and Bill did great work for twenty-five years, and after the long partnership, they decided to sell their business. They were both getting older and ready for the next chapter of their lives. The next chapter for Sam was to start his own executive advising/business coaching business. He had built the real estate business from the ground up and wanted to help C-level executives and their teams who are successful but stuck, get unstuck and on the path of growth. His business spanned all avenues of business because Sam prided himself on knowing the inner workings of business as a whole. He started White Hall Business Coaching in his fiftieth year, and for two years had built it up to an exceptionally respectable twenty or so clients.

Sam had always been a people person. It was what helped him in the real estate business and what set him up to be a success in the consulting business. He had the keen ability to meet people on their level, and to read and guide them to places that they never truly believed they could go.

* * * *

Jacob got to his desk earlier than usual on the day Sam was set to visit. Before hanging up with him a few days earlier, Sam had tasked Jacob with producing his business plans (current and past), and the organizational chart for his company. This is why Jacob was extra early to the office that day. He had a very adept vision when planning his business, knowing exactly where he wanted it to go and what he wanted it to accomplish. His fault was that he never really put it on paper. For today's meeting, this was going to be a problem.

He took out a yellow legal pad. The yellow gave him a sense of comfort that the white legal pads could not. And, today, he needed all the comfort he could get. As he bent his knees to sit in his chair, he removed his Titleist from his front right pocket and rolled it around his right hand. After allowing the familiar ball to calm some of his nerves, he placed it on his desk next to his yellow legal pad. He began to scratch down his plan, his organizational chart, and then eventually put his pen down. He got up and walked to the office kitchen to grab a second cup of coffee.

As he lowered himself back into his chair, he sighed deeply with frustration. The problem was, he *knew* what he wanted for this assignment, but the disconnect between his brain and his right arm was strong. The words would not get onto the paper the right way. The outline of his business would not get on the paper the way he wanted it to. Nothing was coming to him.

With half of the legal pad crumpled in the wire trash can beside him, and half of his morning nearly gone, he scribbled down a very unorganized and barely legible organizational chart. His business plan was even less of an acceptable document. He exhaled, combed through some old files hoping to find his original documents with the same information, and only came up with two of the four he needed.

He organized them into separate years and cleaned off his desk so as to at least give the appearance that he had a speck of clarity. He got in touch with his employees in the conference room, explaining what the rest of the day held for TBM. He had informed everyone yesterday of Sam's pending arrival, but this meeting was about details.

As noon approached, every employee was eagerly awaiting his or her guest. Jacob sat at his desk, hands beginning to sweat, as he tried to predict how it would go. Eventually, the phone on his desk buzzed and his office manager said, "Jacob, I have a Sam Cobb here for you."

"Thanks, Jacki. Send him in."

After the initial introductions again, this time in person, they both made their way to the conference room which was stocked with bottled water and fresh notepads. Jacob was nervous.

"Sam, I … I … I'm not sure where to begin. I love my career and my company, but I'm stuck. Frozen. Lost. I don't know what to do, how to think or what's next..."

"Jacob," Sam interrupted with a firm yet empathic voice, "first, I want you to take a deep breath and relax. I'm sure nothing is as bad as it seems and, even if it is, nothing is happening that cannot be repaired. Some of it may take longer than others, but I promise you this: everything is closer than it seems."

"That's a relief," Jacob said as he began to finally crack a smile and release the first hint of a nervous laugh.

"Jacob, listen to me, you have built a strong business, but you're stuck. It is as simple as that. What that means is it is time for you and the company to evolve to its next level. That starts with many things, but mostly your culture and people. This is where we will begin. How does that sound?"

"That sounds great, Sam," Jacob responded.

"Jacob, I need you to trust me and be very open and honest in answering the questions I ask you. We are going to dive deep into your business and the culture of what makes up your company. Don't hold back. There is *no* judgment here, but if you don't put it all on the table, we can't grow to the extent we want to." This man was endearing himself to Jacob with every word he spoke.

"Sam, you got it." Jacob was beginning to feel much more comfortable with what was happening at this point. Jacob's instincts told him that this was the real deal and this was going to create the change needed to grow his company. And himself. Jacob began to relax more in his chair and allowed himself to get excited for what was about to come.

Sam began to write a few things down on his notepad. After two minutes of writing, he looked up and said, "Jacob, are you ready to get started?"

"Yes," Jacob said with much anticipation and a small hint of fear, though the fear was subsiding quickly.

"Alright. First, I want you to tell me what you want to accomplish by working with me. Then we'll start with some follow-up questions. So, what do you want to accomplish?"

"Sam, I don't exactly know, and I need you to help guide me there, but I need a long-term plan, an immediate plan, systems, processes, marketing and branding, a deeper culture, people who love coming to work and who are motivated to work and..."

Sam again cut in, "Jacob, it sounds like you want it all?" They both laughed. "How about if I take the lead, and we'll take this step-by-step. I'll start and keep you in the know of what each next step will be in the building of our business roadmap."

"Roadmap?" Jacob asked, a bit confused by this terminology.

"Yes, a roadmap. We are going to build you a business plan roadmap. It will map out everything and more of what you talked about earlier. I know exactly how we will get you there, but let's start at the beginning. How does that sound?"

"But, Sam, what about ..." Jacob started before being quickly interrupted.

"Slow down. Let's not jump the gun. One piece at a time," Sam said. "I got this. Let's start with those questions I was talking about. I asked you to bring an organizational chart to our meeting. Do you have that?"

Jacob handed it to Sam, a little ashamed of the disorganized organizational chart. It didn't look official—more of a last-minute legal pad mess.

Sam and Jacob made their way through the jumbled legal pad organizational chart and then concluded their lunch meeting. It was not ideal for Jacob, and as Sam was

leaving he felt embarrassed. Sam would be back on
Monday for his initial review of everyone in the company.

Jacob made his way back to his office, and gathered
himself for a dinner tonight he had been looking forward to
for a month.

Chapter 13: Guys Night Out

You are the average of the five people you spend the most time with.
- Jim Rohn

As the week was ending following Sam's initial visit to Jacob's company, Jacob tried to grasp the enormity of what his new coach was going to put into place. In what was mostly his youthful ignorance—maybe it was arrogance—he never thought that within five years his business would be in this position. The thought initially made anger and frustration rise within him, upset that he could not do this on his own. So far, he *had* done everything on his own, with support from a great group of people. But, none of those people had delved into his business and given him guided steps and action plans on what he *should* be doing. What he *had* to be doing.

Now, he was meeting with a business coach and being given instructions about correcting the culture *he* had built in his business. After a quick, ten-second trip through frustration, he remembered his mother's words—and those of Dr. Marc, too—about accepting help. He knew he needed it, and the heat of anger that he felt rising in his face began to subside.

As his meeting with Sam ended, Jacob went back to his office, optimistic about his past hour with Sam. With his company's anniversary quickly approaching, Jacob called Deborah Morah, the owner of Deborah's Chocolates. She made the best and most decorative gift baskets around. Over the years, Jacob came to know Deborah quite well. In fact, she was the type of woman who was like a mother to everyone who met her. Deborah and his parents grew up in the same area and, on the day Jacob's office opened, a gift basket from his favorite chocolate supplier arrived, compliments of his father. Ever since, Jacob has used his connection in the candy industry to send baskets to clients after they closed a deal. It was his way of saying congratulations.

The reason for his call to Deborah on this afternoon was different. He wanted to arrange something for his employees. As he sat at his desk with the phone to his ear, he now knew the answer to the question that had haunted him for the past week: Why celebrate?

The reason he did not feel like celebrating was his own doing. It was because of the culture that he created. The problem was not his employees. They had been doing all they could under the circumstances. As Sam told him, "You *must* take care of your employees. You *must* make them feel important." He felt he could start with a small gesture to say congratulations and thanks for sticking with me, like a gift basket from Deborah.

"Good afternoon, Deborah's Chocolates. Deborah speaking. How may we help you today?" the voice on the other end of the line said. The words were delivered with as much excitement as someone who had just won the Powerball Lottery. This was classic Deborah—the most fun-loving, carefree, overly congenial person Jacob had ever met. It was because of this demeanor that Jacob trusted her. He felt safe with her, and he was glad to be her client.

"Hey Deborah, it's Jacob Wengrow."

"Oh. My. Goodness. Jacob, stinkin' Wengrow! How in the world are you, boy?" she said.

"I'm doing alright. Think you could do me a favor?" he asked. He loved talking to Deborah, but soon he had a very important dinner he needed to get to. One that he hadn't missed in almost ten years.

"Sure, hon, I can do anything for you!" she said, very excited to hear from him.

"Great! Our five-year anniversary is coming up next week. Do you think I could get gift baskets made for my employees? They can all be the same, but I'd like three of them to be a little extra-special for my department heads. Can you do that?"

"Can I do that?" she repeated loudly. Jacob knew what was coming next. "Is the Pope Catholic? Of course, I can do that! When do you need it by?"

"Could I have it for Friday—one week from today?" he asked.

"Ab-so-lutely! That won't be a problem at all. I'll even help deliver them. I wouldn't mind seeing you once in awhile, you know?"

"I know, I miss you too. Thanks again, Deborah. I'll talk to you next week to confirm plans?" He truly was not trying to push her off the phone, and hoped he wasn't coming across that way.

"Sounds great. Talk to you soon, Jacob," she said, and then hung up the phone.

* * * *

As the quitting hour quickly approached, Jacob gathered his things. Tonight he wasn't eating dinner alone like he usually did. And, he wasn't meeting Joanna either. The two of them had quickly gelled, and they enjoyed many wonderful evenings together as their work schedules had allowed. This week, though, she was out of town for a conference. He would be hanging out with the boys tonight.

Tonight was Boys Night—a monthly gathering with his closest friends: AC, Fish, Dylan, Dan, and Frank. But first, he had one person he had to talk to: Joanna Leigh.

Jacob tossed his brown leather briefcase behind the driver seat of his car, hopped in and dialed Joanna's number before even starting the car. For the past few weeks, they had talked nearly every day and gone out as often as they could. It had only been a couple weeks, but Jacob knew one thing: he liked this girl. A lot.

Joanna was different from any of the other girls he had ever been with. She captivated him with her stories and stole his train of thought with even the slightest of smiles. She was different, and Jacob was enthralled.

On the way to the Punch Bowl Social, a fun and dynamic meeting place for group dinners, Jacob lost himself in conversation with Joanna. They talked about how their week went and about plans for the weekend. She knew all about this new adventure he was on with his business coach and asked about that, while he told her about his idea of giving a gift to his employees. Joanna agreed it was a great idea. They reluctantly hung up the phone with each other as Jacob parked. He told her that he'd try to shoot her a text at some point during the evening. Otherwise, they'd for sure talk tomorrow.

"I'd like that," she said. Jacob smiled as he pressed the *end* button on his cell phone. He could not help but smile as he walked into the Punch Bowl Social.

* * * *

This was Jacob's first time at Punch Bowl Social, and he was impressed by the open architecture inside, the large dining room to the left and the long stretch of bars, tables, and even a bowling alley to the right.

What a typical place for us to meet, he thought with a laugh. He was excited to hang out with these guys tonight.

This was a dinner that Jacob looked forward to every month. All six of the guys coming tonight had been friends since before they could drive. They had played Little League baseball together, ran some school playgrounds, and all graduated from high school and college together.

Once a month, they got together to keep the fires of their friendship burning. Tonight was going to be a great night, and Jacob knew it from the moment that he walked into the Punch Bowl Social. As he gazed beyond the bars, he noticed Fish and AC sitting at one of the high-top tables next to the full-length glass window with a perfect view of pedestrian traffic on Broadway Street.

"Hey there, fellas," Jacob said as he approached the two at the table.

"Well, look who it is!" said Fish, the jokester of the group. "Grab a seat and order a drink," he instructed.

"Hey, Jakey!" AC shouted, knowing how much Jacob hated the nickname when someone other than his mother used it.

"So, that's how the night is going to go? It's good to see you bastards, too," Jacob came back quickly. "Where's everyone else?"

"Well, Dylan is stuck in traffic on I-75. Dan just parked and will be in here any minute. And, well, you know Frank. He's always late for everything. So they'll be here." As Fish finished his answer, a cute, petite blonde, wearing the official Punch Bowl Social tank top, shorts and low-top Chuck Taylors, approached the table.

"Hey guys, I'm Lacey, I'll be taking care of you tonight. Can I get you started with something to drink?" Her voice was attractively raspy.

"Bourbon on the rocks, two green olives, please," Jacob responded as Fish and AC both told her that they were still milking their first beer.

"Same ol Jake. You've been drinking that same damn drink since college. What gives, man?" AC said.

"Just like what I like. Why fix what's not broken?" was Jacob's simple reply.

Fish and AC launched into reminiscing and laughing about many of the same memories they always laughed about while they waited for the others to arrive. It didn't matter that many of the references and jokes were from twenty years ago. They were still just as funny to all of them.

"Alright, alright. New subject. How about that waitress? She's right up your alley, Jacob. You know, now that we're all married. You're the only one that has a chance," Fish reminded him.

"As if you had a chance, even *if* you weren't married," Jacob laughed and lifted his drink to the boys. "I'm not interested, though. Not tonight." As he finished, Dylan and Dan walked in together.

"Looks like the traffic finally cleared. Hey, guys!"

"What's going on, boys?" Dan, the most excitable one of the group, said, "What's it take for someone to get a drink around here?" He signaled for Lacey, and she came over, giving Jacob his swill, and soon she was back with drinks for the rest of them. As they dug through some appetizers, Frank eventually arrived, and the old gang was complete.

* * * *

Whenever the boys got together, it seemed as though the hands on the clock would fly around at high speed. The time passed so quickly that, before they knew it, they had been there for something like four hours. It was always this easy, though. These guys, the five sitting around this table with Jacob, were his best friends in the world. They knew everything about each other. Whenever they needed each other, there were never any questions asked.

It was Frank who asked the question that Jacob dreaded the most.

"Jacob, how's work going?"

He knew that he could tell them everything, but did he want to? He never liked being the center of attention, nor did he ever want to ruin their one meeting a month. Finally, he just blurted, "It's okay." He knew it wouldn't pass as an acceptable answer—they were good at prying—but he hoped they would skip over it. They didn't.

"Okay? Um, what's going on?" Fish, not joking around this time, demanded. "Jacob, what's up man? You know we are here for this exact reason. Shoot us straight."

"Well, uh, things aren't good," Jacob said as he twirled the olives floating in his drink with his thin black straw. He wasn't looking up.

Fish snapped his fingers underneath Jacob's nose and said, "Hey. We're up here. Let's talk. What's going on?" Jacob looked up from his drink, and noticed that all ten eyes were directly on him. His friends were the best. They genuinely were interested in what was going on. And that felt nice.

"Sorry, guys, I hate to be the downer here. Just been a rough couple of months. No, at least a half a year. I haven't talked much about it because I thought I would just come out of it; but, it's been a rough six months."

That was the honest answer. The best answer he could give them. He proceeded to tell them about how he felt like he was spinning his wheels, how he had met Dr. Marc through Aria, and then, the big reveal spilled out.

"It's gotten to the point where I've even enlisted the help of a business coach." He went back to twirling the olives, a feeling of defeat rushing over him.

That was until Frank put his hand on his left shoulder. "Dude, that's great."

"What? How could that be great?" wondered Jacob out loud to his buddies.

"You're getting help." They all nodded in a synchronized manner that was strangely comforting to Jacob. "Sometimes, Jacob, we are too close to situations to realize the solution. Bringing someone in can only help you. The question is, are you willing to get the help? It was a good start to hire him, but are you going to *listen* to him?"

It was an honest question. And, he thought, one that Jacob thought he knew the answer to after one meeting with Sam.

"I think I am. I don't really have a choice. But, you guys know, I have always done everything myself. My parents didn't have a lot, so I worked to put myself through college. I didn't really have help starting TBM. It's just not in my nature, I guess."

"Ah, but that's the thing," AC cut in, "the moment you start to *try* to accept help, you're not only going to improve your business, but you'll also grow it. We all know that's going to happen, you're too talented for it not to. But once you learn to accept help, you'll also be bettering yourself, growing who *you are.* In the end, isn't that worth all of it?"

Everyone at the table took a silent pause at the truth that was just placed before them. Though no one spoke, everyone knew that AC was right.

"Damn," Jacob eventually cut the silence, "you're right. I was not in the best of moods coming here. I'm nervous about what Sam—my business coach—is going to do or ask of me. But in the end, AC, you hit the nail on the head." The doubts, in that moment, grew wings and lifted themselves from Jacob's shoulders. Now, he could enjoy the rest of the night with his friends.

The boys paid their tabs, shook hands, and gave the obligatory bro hug. As they made their way to their cars, each of them promised to check up on Jacob before they met again next month. He knew they were good for it. He was grateful for his friends' advice. He desperately needed it.

On the drive home, Jacob wasn't thinking about his brokerage firm, Sam or even the great night he had just spent with his best friends. There was only one thought that kept creeping back into his mind: Joanna.

Chapter 14: Organizing the Chaos

The secret of getting ahead is getting started.
- Mark Twain

As the new week began, Jacob's nerves were through the roof. Thinking of his upcoming meeting with Sam made his palms sweat and left him on edge. He was having trouble wrapping his mind around the fact that *he* was the problem. How had he become *that* guy? The same guy he always vowed he would never become. The same guy he would judge and criticize at his old companies. He was disappointed that, not only had he become this person but also that no one had the kindness to point it out to him. Had he become that aloof and unapproachable? *Who is the guy I'm looking at when I look in the mirror?* he thought.

He sat and reflected at his desk as he waited for Sam to cross the threshold into his office. He was considering all of the coincidences that had taken place recently for him to end up with what will surely be an intense conversation with Sam. Thankfully, Aria set him on the road to transformation. Aria, Dr. Marc, Sharon, Adam, and even Michael all had played a part in creating this moment for him. He was scared, vulnerable, but generally he was grateful that this moment had come.

As he reflected, he remembered a TED talk by Brené Brown, in which she discussed "Daring Greatly." To do this, she taught, you must put yourself in the arena of vulnerability to grow. Jacob felt as if he was doing that. He was more vulnerable in this moment than he could ever recall.

He then remembered a book he read many years ago, called *Seat of the Soul* by Gary Zukav. It discussed how the ideal soul is where the personality ends and the soul begins. Jacob knew he was not in alignment with that statement. Life had become crisscrossed. With life's craziness and him always running full speed ahead, he had lost balance and forgot many of the lessons he had learned throughout the years.

Was his meeting with Sam going to be the same? Would they meet and then the lessons fade into the dark recesses of his brain? Would he realize, years later, that he forgot most of what they talked about and what he had learned? He was hoping this time would be different and determined that indeed it would be. As he was finishing his thoughts, the *click* of the door echoed through his quiet office, and Jacob noticed the well-dressed, middle-aged man standing before him.

"Hello, Sam, nice to see you again," Jacob said as he shot his hand toward Sam with the firm handshake his dad and grandfather taught him was so important to have. *Shake it straight, firm, and look them in the eye,* his dad would say. *Show them how confident and strong of a businessman you are from the minute they meet you,* his grandfather instructed. "I'm so glad you could come in today, Sam, thank you. I need you. My company needs you in some ways I know; mostly in ways I don't yet understand."

"Jacob, it's my pleasure. I'm looking forward to our meeting today. I think great things are ahead," Sam responded with a smile. It was a trusting smile, and the fear that had gripped Jacob earlier in the day slowly faded away.

"Thank you," Jacob said with an insecure smile. He felt as if he didn't know where to go or what to do. There were so many questions in his head. He didn't know where to begin. He and Sam made their way to the conference room, and after some small pleasantries Sam began the meeting.

"Okay, let's start here. Tell me about each person, their strengths and weaknesses, their role and responsibilities, and if they are a fit for the organization," Sam said.

"A fit?" Jacob asked, but in his mind he thought, *This guy is already talking about firing people? Where is he going with all of this?* The fear began to rear its ugly head back into the conference room.

"Jacob, snap out of it!" Sam said with a snap of his fingers. "I need you present, here in this moment. It's important for me to get my own perspective of your people from *your* perspective. I'll get my own when I talk to them one-on-one. I want the truth, no fluff. Remember, open and honest. So tell me about your people. Are they a fit?" Sam again questioned him.

Sam began to look over the organizational chart, handed to him the past Friday, going line-by-line, person-by-person. He waited in silence, and when he did not receive a reply he looked up. Jacob was sitting across from him, but his palms were pressed against his eyes, and he was rubbing them in a circular motion. He had no idea where to begin, or with whom.

As Sam and Jacob sat around the conference room table, Sam continued to ask about Jacob's team. This was not intended to be a deep information-gathering mission, but was supposed to focus around two specific questions:

- What is each person's key role and responsibility supposed to be?
- How does that person affect the culture of your business?

Jacob proceeded to tell Sam about the rest of his team with just a few details as their meeting continued.

Sam was listening for how connected Jacob was to the company, as well as to his people. Sam had seen this time and time again throughout the years: CEOs of companies big and small all disconnected from the daily workings and the people involved in them. Somewhere along their way, many of them all seem to disconnect from their mission, as well: their company's purpose and culture lost, if they ever had one to begin with.

Sam often told the same story Michael Jordan told in his book, *I Can't Accept Not Trying*, about Larry Bird. By mastering the fundamentals—and practicing those fundamentals—he was able to be one of the best athletes of his time and continue to grow because he understood the fundamentals of his craft.

He tells of how many younger athletes who came out of high school or ignored the fundamentals could only get to a certain level because they did not have the foundation to grow from. It was a constant theme for Sam as he met with various high-level executives in different companies. These were CEOs who grew too fast or did not have the proper planning in place and just *winged* it. They get to a point where they can't grow, and they need someone like

Sam to bring back the fundamentals and be the assistant coach in growing the business.

Sam knew his place; he was the guy behind the guy. He did not need or want the glory. It was enough for him to lend his years of experience and let others shine even if they were his ideas they were implementing. He thought that these smart and hardworking people were building companies, but they weren't. They were stuck, and he was honored to give them the boost they needed to get unstuck. He was the expert from afar who came in and made magic happen—made *success* happen—because he was not a corporate guy. He had a knack for seeing and hearing things differently than most everyone else. This was his special talent and the value he brought to companies. That, plus the ability to influence change and action in CEOs and their teams. He loved what he did and never let his ego get in the way.

In a way, he was like Mary Poppins. When things get rough, he swoops in to analyze, direct, and remedy the matter. This means that everyone can bring their best selves to the company and have a reclaimed pride in what they do again. He connects companies back together, like a puzzle. That is what he found fulfilling—seeing the light come back into the company and watching everyone grow and perform better, more efficiently, more successfully.

Unlike Mary Poppins, however, he sticks around even after the initial four to six months of hard, heavy transformation and recovery. Those who wanted to be held accountable, continue to see the results and move forward in their growth, recognized the value of that. And, those who do not stick to the process, face the consequences of potentially going backwards.

Chapter 15: The People

High expectations are the key to everything.
- Sam Walton

As their meeting continued, Sam said, "Jacob, let's begin by diving deeper into those people you call your leadership team. We'll start with Jacki, your office manager. Tell me about her." Sam was trying to get Jacob's mind off of the gigantic task ahead of setting his business roadmap and onto smaller, more manageable chunks. He had been at this long enough and knew that the only way to eat an elephant is one bite at a time.

"Sam," Jacob began, smiling at the mention of her name. Jacki Vernon had been there from the beginning, and this was a softball that Sam had tossed him. Now, he just had to hit it out of the park. "I couldn't do anything without her. She is the eyes and ears of the company for me. She is not only loyal but also brilliant. She has been with me my entire career and came with me from the other company. I hired her right out of college, and now she basically runs the company with me. Everyone loves her. She is strong with people and numbers, and she always has my back.

"She is a very special person. She has the uncanny ability to get people down to business while still making them laugh. She probably is too qualified for the role, but it allows her the convenience and flexibility to work and raise her two kids, William and Daisy, and her dog, Pretzel. Her husband runs a large tutoring company, so she works for fun and to keep her busy, not for the money. We are lucky to have her. I am lucky to have her. She has a photographic memory, so she remembers and knows everything. So, in return, I forget nothing. Or so I thought. But, I would have appreciated it if she had told me that everyone in the company hates me," Jacob said with a smirk of humor and a tinge of embarrassment.

"Jacob, I'm sure nobody hates you, but it does sound like you are misunderstood from the tone I hear in your voice. Don't mistake this: those feelings begin with you—your tone, the words you use, your physiology, your humor, all of it when in the workplace. You need to ask yourself why your number one person in the office did not come to you with this. And maybe that answer is that you've become a tyrant of sorts, and completely unapproachable. It reminds me of the scene in the movie *Hook*, where Wendy tells Peter, 'Peter, you've become a pirate.' He had lost his way, and so have you. You must understand that everything you do, I'm talking ninety-five percent of how you walk, talk, glare, laugh, and work is setting the bar, the culture, the standards, and the inner workings of your company. There is no denying that. You must own this leadership role and responsibility. You must own it today, or we cannot continue our work."

Jacob looked like he had just seen a ghost.

"Ninety-five percent, Sam? Don't these people get it? Don't they have any personal initiative? Don't they want to grow? Don't they have opinions and thoughts of their own? Are you telling me that every fucking thing I do they are watching me like flies on shit?" Jacob was irritated at the level of responsibility that was on his shoulders and needed to vent about it, not necessarily caring what Sam thought.

"Yes. Everyone has some level of personal initiative. But most people, whether they know it or not, choose to work for a company because of the culture. That culture is created by the leaders of the company. That's you. Period. The end. Your team wants to follow an eagle, not a pigeon that shits over everything and everyone." Sam finished in a firm voice, "Got it?"

Minutes passed that felt like hours. Jacob looked directly at Sam and replied, "Got it. I hear you, and I own it."

"Good. Let's continue ..."

"I have three managers who oversee different parts of the company," Jacob said somewhat confidently and at least as sheepishly.

"Tell me more ..." Sam said.

"For starters, there is the head of sales, Doug, who is a bit weak. He is good and in the beginning was doing great, but then got a bit burnt out. I decided to promote him to head of sales, and as I'm telling you this, I'm realizing that was a mistake. I didn't want to lose him back then, but in hindsight, I would be better off today if I let him leave when he was burnt out," Jacob said.

"See how this works, Jacob? When you simply take the executive time to discuss some of these things, the answers just spill out."

"Damn. Now I'm frustrated at what could have been today. If what you say is right about the leader setting the pace, then between this guy and me, the people under him must be working at fifty percent capacity."

"Probably lower, actually," Sam corrected.

A look of personal disappointment came over Jacob's face. "Why didn't I have the courage to make that decision over three years ago?"

"Jacob, let that go immediately. You cannot live in the past. You cannot change it. We are talking about today and looking forward. I will not let you live in the past with regret. Listen up: do you know the best time to plant a tree?"

"When, Sam?"

"Now. Now, Jacob is the best time to plant a tree. You are planting a tree today for tomorrow. Life and business are easy in hindsight. Moving forward there will be less regret because you are putting a stronger team in place to guide you. It's not to replace you or make decisions for you, but to guide you. Get it?" Sam asked.

"Yes, for the most part," Jacob said, still fluttering in his disappointment and trying to make the connection between trees and business.

"You will."

"As I'm talking to you right now, I know Doug Goodwise needs to go. He is not a fit for the organization. On top of that, he and I have never seen eye to eye. He is always pushing my buttons and..." Jacob trailed off, knowing what he wanted to say, but trying to avoid it.

"And what?" Sam prodded.

"He is always talking shit about me and making me look bad," sputtered Jacob, knowing that his face was turning red with anger.

"How long has this been going on?" Sam followed up.

"Since he started. I still promoted him because I was scared if I let him go, I would lose others, and I felt I needed him to grow the company." Jacob started to feel foolish. He really sounded incompetent hearing the words himself. *Who is the man I am looking at when I look in the mirror? Do I even recognize him anymore?* he thought to himself.

Sam responded with a simple piece of advice. "Jacob, let me give you a piece of advice right now. Don't ever make a decision out of fear or because you feel desperate. It will get you nowhere, fast. Very fast. No one can take away your vision, your passion, or your company. You are an entrepreneur, and if everyone left your company today, you would rebuild. You are a builder. I know this is much easier said than done, but it's time for you to take back control of your company. Get it?"

The words rang true, and now that anger started to turn to deep-seated nervousness. Like that football player feels in the pit of his stomach as he stands in the tunnel waiting to run on the field. It was adrenaline, and Jacob liked the fuel building up in his insides.

"Got it," he replied quickly and confidently.

"What are you going to do about Doug?" came the follow-up question.

"I think I have to let him go," Jacob said less confidently, still feeling the fear grip his shoulders and rest itself upon him.

"You may be right, but let me see how my one-on-one with him goes first. Deal?" Sam asked.

"Deal."

* * * *

Sam took copious notes as he listened to Jacob review everyone in the company, specifically his leadership team. Jacob struggled with some and spoke easily about others.

Jacob spent about ninety minutes talking to Sam about the people in his company. Much of the time was spent reviewing his three managers: Doug, the Sales Manager, Jacki, the Office Manager, and Jamie, the Marketing Director. Each of them had a team under them. Doug had a team of four salespeople, Jamie had two people under her, and Jacki had two administrators under her. Also, there was one technology person. That meant thirteen people worked at TBM and Sam made fourteen.

As the conversation came to an end, Jacob looked spent. He turned to Sam and said, "Sam, I don't think I have ever taken the time to do this. I mean really sit down and talk about my company in this way. I have read about taking executive time to plan—and many coaches have told me, too—but I never do. I always plan on doing it and think the idea is great, but have never formed the habit or chose to have the discipline. Now I regret that."

"Jacob, don't look back with regret. Stop that now. You did the best you could with the tools you had to date. Moving forward you will start looking at things differently. Your perspective will begin to change. Do you think you can change the past?"

Taken aback by such a seemingly obvious question, Jacob responded, "No, of course not. That's ridiculous."

"No, it's not. You can change the past. Think about something that happened in the past—don't tell me what it is, but think about the situation. Now think about how many different perspectives and opinions there could have been for that situation. Now remember your own opinion and perspective. Got it Jacob? Got it in your head?"

"Yes, Sam, I got it."

"Okay. Now change your perspective on any part of it. Take a minute and think of someone else's perspective. See it through different lenses for one minute. Can you do that?"

"Yes, I can." They sat there for a minute while Jacob did the exercise. Jacob took a deep breath and said, "Wow, Sam. I get it. I changed my perspective and everything changed along with it. Is it that easy?"

"If you want it to be. It's your choice. We have choices every day. We have the option to fully and completely believe the stories we tell ourselves, the stories we inherited, and the stories we created and lived through. Do you believe you have choices, Jacob?"

"Of course I do, but sometimes I feel so rushed. I can't make the choices I need to make because I don't know if I trust my instincts," Jacob said, starting to hang his head.

"Jacob, we are going to change that. If you are open to change and growth, we will get you listening to your gut and making decisions based on your instincts and heart. We will get you out of your own head."

"Sam, are you telling me not to use my head?"

"That's exactly what I'm telling you," confirmed the coach.

"I don't understand?" Jacob said, now more confused.

"You will—just be patient. Deal?" Sam asked, smiling.

With anxious frustration, Jacob simply responded, "Deal."

Sam continued to lay out the blueprint for Jacob. "As we go through this process, I will fix everything for you. I will get your company back on track. You have to put forth the effort and hard work to make it happen and take action on everything we talk about. As so does your team.

"I will also help to fix the connection between your people and your company. You won't recognize your culture three months from now, and six months from now you will look back and won't believe you were ever in this place you are today. I am going to connect your gut and your heart and make you a better decision maker who has strong convictions and solid confidence, with a humility necessary to lead people. I am going to get your people in sync with the company's vision and goals along with their own goals. Everyone is going to start bringing their best ideas to work and turn their work into a passionate career.

"It will never be perfect. You don't want it to be perfect, that would be no fun, but we are going to put systems, processes, and methodologies in place, so everyone knows the assembly line of what needs to get done. They will know who is doing it and where they fit and how they matter in the organization. You will start to see more smiles, which is one way you will be able to measure the results. You will laugh more and people will choose to proactively talk to you instead of shying away from you. The energy of your entire office will begin to change. Simply, Jacob, you will feel the difference.

"But, don't kid yourself: it takes *a lot* of work. Everyone must do it, and everyone must see you vulnerable, gritty, and getting your hands dirty, as the leader they want to follow. I will guide you as you evolve into that person. I know you can be him. He is inside you. You are a leader, a builder, and an influencer. Now, it's time to take all those qualities, package them up, and start inspiring people. It's time to get everything together for growth and start growing your people. How does that sound, Jacob?" Sam asked confidently.

"It sounds like a dream come true."

Sam continued, "It's not just a dream. Now, it's a reality, Jacob. I want you to also know this right now: I am here to guide you, support you, teach you, but never enable you. I am going to push you and hold you accountable. Our conversations won't always be easy for you. You need to always hear things with the right ears because my intentions are all positive. In many cases, I will be the messenger. There will be days when you will be upset because of what we talk about or how I push you, but you have to rise above it. Growth is not easy, and you need to step up for your own growth, your people, and the company. Do we have a deal?"

"You got it, Sam, I promise," Jacob offered, as confidence was beginning to creep into him.

"One last thing, Jacob. I want you to know I will never get in your way. This is your company. I am the guy behind the guy. I never need or want credit. I never need the accolades and, frankly, I will never tell people I worked with you and your company. I have a strict policy about this. I don't talk about my clients with anyone. However, feel free to talk about me. I only grow my business through introductions. I am here to essentially be in the background. It's all about you, your people, and the company. Get it?"

"Got it, Sam. Thank you for your kindness. I'm sitting here listening, and it's as if you are the first person to ever give it to me straight. You know, tell me how it is and have my back. I don't think even my own parents ever showed this much faith in me, let alone took the time to teach me what you are mapping out for me. Thank you, Sam, I'm excited for all of this."

"Well, thank *you* for the kind words, Jacob, but please *do not* think I am God and can walk on water! I'm not and I never have, nor will I. I am far from perfect, but my coaching superpower can make things happen. I don't want you to get Cab Driver Syndrome when you work with me."

"What's that?" Jacob said laughing.

"You know how when you are on vacation, you get a cab driver or an Uber driver who is the greatest and you have the best conversation in the world with them? You get out of the car after a twelve-minute drive and say, 'Wow, that guy is the greatest guy in the world. He really gets me.'"

"For sure, Sam. Happens all the time."

"Well, right now, I'm the cab driver, and that feeling that I'm perfect will dissipate soon. I actually need you to throw it away, because our work can't get gritty if you feel that way; I'm a normal human with many flaws and I'm here to help you grow the business. We on the same page?"

"Yes, Sam, we're on the same page."

"Okay, Jacob, then let's start the interviews. I want to start with the leadership team. Let's start with Doug."

"Oh boy! Let the games begin. I'll get him." Jacob was giddy, as he knew most likely what was in store for Doug.

Just breathe, Jacob, calm down. I got this, he murmured to himself assuredly.

Jacob left the conference room to go get Doug for his one-on-one with Sam.

* * * *

Minutes later, Doug walked into the conference room with big, blue, insecure eyes. He was looking down as he shook Sam's hand firmly, with a controlling turn to the right. He was in his mid-fifties and gave off the energy of someone who had made many wrong choices and was not where he wanted to be in his life. It seemed that he wanted to make sure that everyone around him paid the price for his mistakes.

With a smile and twinkle in his eye, Sam stood up and shook Doug's hand, greeting him jovially, "Doug, great to meet you. I'm Sam. How are you?"

Sam has the innate ability to read people from the moment he meets them. He does not judge them but can assess them quickly. In those few moments, he creates questions in his mind to bring the best and worst out of that person in order to get a full picture of how they would fit, evolve, and grow as individuals and benefit the company.

Within minutes of talking to Doug, Sam knew Doug was not a fit for the organization. He had a bitter edge to him and was not a team player. Sam knew that Doug's time at TBM was going to be over soon. Sam knew it was time for Doug to move on. Doug felt the same way, but would never pull the trigger. Jacob had to do it himself. He needed the freedom to allow his company to grow without Doug, and also allow Doug the opportunity to find a job that he enjoys going to, each and every day.

After finishing with Doug, Sam caught up with Jacob to fill him in on his observations and his recommendation that Doug be let go. Then Sam asked to have Jamie come into the conference room. When Jamie walked in with the typical bounce in her step, Sam reached to shake her hand. Jamie pushed his hand away and gave him a welcoming hug. That was Jamie—always the optimist, and always a hugger.

She spoke first. "Sam, it is so nice to meet you. I have heard so many great things about you, and we are so excited you are here to help us get cleaned up and growing. I love this company, and I love what I do, but we have lost our way. Jacob has lost his way a bit, but I know we can find our way back because everyone's heart is in the right place," she said.

Sam smiled, happy that Jamie was so open and such a solid communicator. He knew he would get some good information from her about this company's situation and issues so he could best facilitate the change and growth it needed.

"Jamie, tell me how you got to TBM?" he asked.

"Ah, well, Sam, I have always loved marketing, strategy and brand management. I went to school at MSU—GO GREEN!—and got a marketing degree. Frankly, when I graduated, I was a bit lost. I couldn't find a company that would give me the freedom to be as creative as I wanted to be. Luckily my parents, who are both attorneys and share a practice, are Jacob's attorneys. Jacob uses them as advisors. About five years ago when Jacob was starting the company, he was telling them that he needed a marketing person and *boom!* They made the introduction, and I was hired.

"I knew it was risky to come aboard with a relatively new company, but Jacob believed so much in marketing and told me I could be as creative as I wanted to be to constantly get the message out for the company, employees, listings, track record, and so on. I knew it was a creative fit and I knew I could bring my best self to the table," she explained.

Jeff and Linda Fairway had been Jacob's attorneys for many years. They were top advisors for many of the elite companies and families, not only locally, but around the country. If you were a client of Fairway Law Offices, people knew you meant business. Jeff and Linda were like parents to Jacob. They never forgot his birthday, his work anniversary, or any other occasion in between. They were always there to give him advice—legal, business, or personal. Many times he relied on them as parents and just the sound of their voice would put him at ease. He often called to give them updates about the company, so they were always in the loop.

He also sought their approval, guidance, and thoughtful encouragement, which always seemed to keep him going forward confidently and staying strong in his decisions. Many times, he tweaked his plans or changed course depending on their opinions or advice. They had been warning him that he was on a bumpy road and encouraged him to get a business coach more than once. Yes, they told him it was time to look at his company through different lenses; but he was too stubborn to hear it. Now, however, the student was ready, and the teacher had arrived.

"It's always great how fate plays a constant role in our lives. Many people dismiss it. I don't, and it sounds like you don't either, Jamie," Sam responded. "Jamie, before we dive into your thoughts on what is going on with the company, tell me your thoughts on marketing, branding, messaging, and other aspects of your job here."

"Well, Sam, business is marketing. Everything is marketing. Marketing is about consistently sending people the message that supports your brand. Branding is what people say about you when you leave the room. Marketing, branding, and messaging all go together hand in hand. That is why I love it so much and why I have so much fun doing it. I am able to take everything we do and everyone we work with and create marketing and branding campaigns around all of it. Today, with social media, I don't have to worry about something not working. If I'm doing a social media campaign and it doesn't work, I change course and don't have to worry about printing costs." She laughed at the simplicity of it all.

"That is an incredible review of marketing and branding. You are spot on, Jamie." Sam responded to her before continuing, "Jamie, tell me what we need to fix in the company."

"Well, Sam, to be completely honest, we first need to fix Jacob's attitude and commitment. We all respect him, but his attitude when he started the company was always so energetic. He was ready to take over the world, and he always infused us with positive energy. We could all feel his passion. Now, he comes in later than he used to and he's flat. He doesn't invigorate us. We can't have a flat leader of the company. We need excitement and we need it from him.

"Also, I've noticed that his commitment is lagging. He used to be in the zone—sharp on every topic that was thrown at him by any client or any employee. Now, he's just indifferent or apathetic—I don't know which one. He can't seem to make a decision with confidence.

"If Jacob were to go back to being the old Jacob, we would have a lot more excitement in the company, and it would be more fun to work here again. Not that it's not fun, it's just not exciting like it used to be." She wasn't mincing words. Her response was honest. Sam never looked up from his notepad and jotted down everything she said.

"Jamie, that was priceless feedback. Exactly the kind of thing I needed to hear. I like the way you think. You are going to be a huge part of the growth and change. Have you ever told Jacob this?" he asked.

"In a way, but not really," she said.

"Jamie, we are going to have a leadership meeting, which you will be part of on Wednesday. I would like you to share that with Jacob. Are you okay with that?"

"Of course. I only want what is best for Jacob and the company. I just don't want to cross any lines and lose my job," she said. She was confident that she wouldn't lose her job, but hesitant because of her loyalty to Jacob.

"If you give someone feedback in the right way—coming from the heart—you don't need to worry about losing your job. If anything, when you provide feedback from that place and the person who is receiving it can't or won't accept it and reacts negatively, you need to determine if that is a place you want to be. Understand?" He looked her right in the eye when asking this question, focusing on the importance of it.

"Yes, I understand." Jamie was taken aback by how direct Sam was to say something that would make her think she should leave if Jacob didn't step up. She realized that Sam was all about looking at the whole picture, and not just Jacob's side of things. Jamie knew it, and she was confident that Sam was going to be the change they were looking for. And this made her excited for the possibilities that lay ahead.

"Jamie, anything else you want to talk to me about?" he asked.

"Sam, I would like to hear more about you—your ideas and where you think we can take the company—but I'm assuming that will be part of the leadership meeting?" she asked.

"Yes," said Sam. He then went on to tell her a little about himself and let her know he would dive into more detail later.

Jamie left the meeting very excited to be part of the growth and desperately needed change in the company. Being in charge of marketing, branding, and messaging, she heard Sam's message loud and clear, both what he was and was not saying.

Chapter 16: The Talk You Need to Walk

People who are unable to motivate themselves must be content with mediocrity, no matter how impressive their other talents.

- Andrew Carnegie

Sam finished his one-on-one talks with each of Jacob's managers, spending about an hour with each of them. Some conversations were more fluid than others, but Sam felt he got a good grasp of each of their talents, complaints about the company and Jacob, their views of the culture, and what they wanted to see in the growth of the organization. Once these were complete, Sam returned to interview each of the remaining employees for thirty minutes each.

There is a big difference between what people say, what they mean, and what Sam hears. Sam's superpower allowed him to hear what was not being said and see what was not being seen or even ignored. With the interviews concluded, Sam gathered back into the conference room, to address his concerns with Jacob.

As he sat at the table waiting for Jacob to arrive, Sam reflected on all the people he talked to and one thing was obvious to him. In the interest of having all the right people in all the right places doing all the right things, there were clearly two people who needed to be let go immediately.

173

Sam realized that proper HR discussions and document filings were most likely not yet done, but there were two people who were so toxic to the current organization that they would surely prevent the positive change that was about to come.

Firing is so hard for people, Sam thought.

Sam tried to teach his clients that letting someone go from a company is an act of kindness and compassion. It doesn't have to be nasty. It can be done in a way that allows both parties to keep their dignity. Even quitting a job takes courage. The same goes for the firing process: it takes courage. It is a huge responsibility to know that you are putting food on a family's table. That, plus having an emotional connection that came from months or years of working together: you know their story, their back story, and their families. Most run from the pain of that alone. The obstacle is the company cannot run from it. It melts from it.

When an employee does not want to be at the company, and you let them go, you are doing them a huge favor. They may not realize it at the moment. But, if the right seat is not available here, that person needs to be set free to find it elsewhere. Their love and passion are as important to them as your growth and success are to you.

What holds many back is they have no Plan B. There is no plan for who will assume those responsibilities. It is an overwhelming notion that paralyzes many.

"As an owner of a company or as someone who runs a division, you have a responsibility to the people who come with their all to give them the working environment they deserve. Remember, you are only as high as your lowest standard. It's not what you preach, it's what you tolerate." Sam would tell his clients this all the time.

"You need to get rid of the toxic people, set them free and set the others free to bring their best selves and their best ideas to the table so they can grow, and the company can grow. Keeping the wrong people around is a disservice to not only you and the company but also the people who depend on you to give them a healthy environment and lead them to their individual greatness," he would add.

Sam knew that it would be difficult for Jacob to fire the employees he was about to recommend; but, Sam had a plan. And he knew it was the right plan for both Jacob and the company.

* * * *

Jacob found that he was very nervous to hear what Sam was about to say. One thing for sure, Sam had a way of delivering information that was firm, direct, and real, but with the inspiration that everything was fixable and possible. They both knew change took a lot of effort, but Sam broke things down into simple next steps and provided solutions to make the difficult seem manageable.

Jacki stopped by the room and saw Sam, greeting him with a smile and said, "Hi Sam!" There was a pep in her step that he did not see earlier. "Great to see you again. We are all excited to see the changes in the company you are going to make."

"Great to see you, Jacki. Thanks. I'm very excited, too," said Sam, with an equally happy tone. "It's going to be fun. A lot of work, but fun," he laughed.

"We're ready for it," Jacki said. "Bring it on!"

Sam found this reaction at most companies that he worked with. Almost everyone loved that change was on the way. At first, many are hesitant, but when they see that they are part of the change and that the leadership wants to change, they hop on board and are willing and ready to do their part.

Typically, Sam's client companies were full of people who were excited. They *wanted* their company leaders to get that much-needed reality check. They *wanted* to see change and to be part of the reshaping that would change the culture and the growth of the company in the future. It was Sam's job to make sure he kept the fire going for them, and to remind them that this building process would take time. He also reminded them that anything is possible.

Finally, Jacob entered the room and shook Sam's hand.

"Hi, Sam, I'm excited and anxious to hear your thoughts."

"I'm excited to give them to you, Jacob." They moved purposefully around the table and sat down. Jacob took a deep breath as he sat across from his coach, Jacob with his coffee and Sam with his room-temperature bottle of water. Sam was a health nut whose signature drink of room-temperature bottled water was always at hand. Just another example of how simple he was.

"Okay, Jacob, you ready?"

"Let's do this, Sam!"

"Jacob, let me first say, you have a tremendous company. The courage you had to start the company on your own was huge, and you should be very proud of yourself. The fact is that it is five years later and still going strong—maybe not as strong as you'd like—but it is alive and around and active in the market. That is a fantastic accomplishment!

"What is happening here is something I see all the time. This is a company that grew a bit too fast, where the owner or CEO starts something on his own and doesn't have a business partner to bounce ideas off of so he is forced to make decisions on his own. Many of them are the right decisions and some may be off track. When you don't have an equal business partner to provide a different perspective, what seems right at the time can end up being wrong in hindsight.

"When you start to veer off track, you can really fall apart quickly. Most CEOs and business owners just don't realize how dangerous a wrong decision can be for a company," Sam finished.

"Dangerous, Sam? This isn't a horror movie," Jacob cut in, trying to relieve a little of the tension he felt in the room.

"Well, Jacob, it actually is to many of the employees I talk to in these types of situations. The obstacle for an owner or a manager is that they *never* will tell you how they or their team truly feel. They will talk around the water cooler about everything and do their best to hide it from their bosses while just 'doing their job.' Most of the time, these people love what they do, but are unhappy with their current company and don't want to start over at another one. So, they deal with it. But, along the way, it creates a toxic culture and a group of people who feel overwhelmed, overworked, and underappreciated. They feel like what they do and say doesn't matter."

"What did you find here?"

"I found all of it. Everything I just mentioned to you. But, the biggest problem in the company is … you."

"Well, please Sam, please cut to the chase," he laughed nervously, "tell me how you really feel."

"Jacob, you have many moving parts and a lot of issues, but I'm here to give you the straight facts. Here are the main issues in your company: your leadership is lacking, your clarity and vision is lacking, your expectations of people are unrealistic, you micromanage people, you are passive-aggressive with your communication, your people are under-trained because you are not investing in training and invested in their growth, they are scared to make a mistake, you interrupt them when they are talking, you don't listen.

"You ask for their opinion, but they know it doesn't matter. You have no standards and measurements so they never really know how they are doing or how they are measured. Lastly, you seem to be disconnected from the company and from them over these past six or so months."

He slid the list over to the other side where Jacob was sitting. As Jacob looked over the list, he responded, "Wow! Can you give me some examples?"

"I can give you many, but the content doesn't matter right now. Do you think this is true? Jacob, I need to know honestly if you agree with this. If you really take a hard look at your business from an outside perspective, can you see what your people see?"

Jacob was flushed with embarrassment and grew nervous that his company was going to close its doors tomorrow and everyone was going to quit. *How could things be this bad*, he thought. But he knew Sam was not a liar and was talented enough to get the real scoop.

"Sam, I ... I ... I ... don't know what to say or think right now, but now that I've digested this for a few minutes, I hate to say it, but yes. They are right. Is everyone going to quit tomorrow?" Jacob felt horrible. This was never the outcome he wanted when he set his sights on starting his company. He wanted just the opposite. As he stared back at Sam across the table, he could not believe the hole he dug himself, his team, and the company into. It was never his intention to get to this place. But, it sure was his intention to make it right.

He continued, "Sam, I hear you. I'm ready for a change. I'm committed to change. When Dr. Marc was at my office and gave me my first dose of reality, it was a wake-up call and ultimately led me to you. I knew something was off, but I didn't know what. I am ready to change, and I want the best not only for myself but also for all the people I work with that give it their all every day. I understand I have a responsibility to give them the platform, the company, and the culture they need to do their best. I'm ready. Where do we begin?"

"Well, Jacob, we begin with putting together the new roadmap for your company, the one we discussed at lunch last Friday. I want to do this with you and your leadership team. Jamie, Jacki, and Doug. Unfortunately, we need to get rid of Doug before we meet as a team. He is not happy here, he hates you, and he's toxic to the organization. The people he manages don't like him or even respect him and if we are in build mode, he needs to go."

"Sam, that sounds so harsh. So cut and dry."

"Because it is, Jacob. I'm not telling you anything you don't know. You should have done it years ago, but you were too scared," Sam corrected him.

"But, Sam, now I don't have a head of sales!"

"Yes, you do. I want you to promote Andy. He will take your company to infinite heights. He is likable and funny. People respect him, and you can build a team around him. I want you to call a recruiter friend of mine to start looking for your new salesperson to build your team. That being said, you should always be recruiting, so you never are in a situation where you have to keep the 'Dougs' in your company. I want you to always be on the lookout for new talent and always have a recruiter looking for you. You can never have enough of the right talent in your company."

"Anyone else?" Jacob asked, now hesitant for the answer.

"Yes, I want you to get rid of Karen in marketing. She brings down the team. She is impossible for Jamie to manage. She brings no value to her division or the company."

"Won't this cause a lot of turmoil in the company?" Jacob asked, curious to hear Sam's reasoning.

"Yes and no. It's all about how you do it and how you deliver the message to the company. For starters, you have a responsibility to your team to provide them the best environment possible with the best platform and people to do their job. Everyone wants to come to work and do a great job. When you—as the leader of the company—put roadblocks in their way, it makes it hard for them. You preach the best but don't back it up with your actions. Remember, Jacob, 'it's not what you preach, it's what you tolerate.' You have tolerated their bad attitudes, poor work product, and bully-type attitudes for too long. Your people want them out more than you do. Once you let them both go and promote Andy all in the same hour, you need to have a company meeting the next morning and deliver the proper message.

"It's this simple: You have them all meet in the conference room and say this:

'*Thank you all for coming. We have parted ways with Doug and Karen. Andy is our new VP, head of sales, and we are in the process of hiring a replacement for Karen through our recruiter, along with one or two more salespeople. With Sam here, we are all very excited for the growth of our company, our culture, and our people. I want you all to know that everyone in this room is secure in their job. That being said, we are going to be working with Sam on many of the things he talked to you about and raising the standards of the company. I expect all of you to rise to the occasion, as I will, and I want you all to hold me to that same expectation. We are building TBM to take it to the next level, and I'm so excited to do it with all of you. If you have any questions, please come talk to me, one on one. Thanks everyone! Have a great day.*'

"You then need to make the rounds and see everyone, one-on-one in the company that day to connect with them about how they are feeling. Ease their worries and answer their questions. You will need to spot check this on a continual basis. My hunch would be that most people will be glad when you get rid of these two. Most people don't like these types of people in an organization. I imagine people will say, 'Thank you, Jacob,' and begin respecting you more for making a decision that is best for the company and morale." Sam finished, then stood from the table and prepared to leave for the day.

Jacob took Sam's advice and let Karen and Doug go the next day. Just as Sam predicted, they both took it well and were glad to be "set free." Neither of them had the courage to quit. So Sam was right: Jacob did them a favor. Jacob then followed up with the company and, overall, everyone was very happy with Jacob's decisions and loved seeing the immediate impact of action and the change that the company had seen since Sam came on board.

Jacob knew he needed to keep his finger on the pulse of the people. He knew others were thinking they might get fired. Overall, however, people seemed more engaged and excited to be part of TBM than he had seen over the last couple of years. *Could this all be the magic of bringing in a business coach?* Jacob wondered.

Since his dinner with Aria, the introduction to Dr. Marc, and now with Sam everything seemed too good to be true, but seemed to be changing for the better. And, not to mention, Joanna was in his life. So many good things were finally happening that Jacob hoped he would not sabotage any of it. He knew he really needed to rely on his new advisors to make the right decisions. He didn't want to veer off the path. He felt as though Sam's guidance would lead him down the yellow brick road and wanted to make sure every step was a step in the right direction.

Now that the team was in place, Jacob, Andy, Jacki, and Jamie were ready for their team meeting with Sam. It would be an eight-hour meeting with Sam to lay the groundwork for the following week of meetings to retool the entire company. The meeting was scheduled for Wednesday and Jacob could hardly wait. Neither could his team.

Part Three:
The Transformation
and Implementation

Chapter 17: The Roadmap

Give me six hours to chop down a tree and I will spend the first four sharpening the axe.
- *Abraham Lincoln*

On that Wednesday, the sun was streaming through the windows as Jacob awoke from a deep, restful sleep. There was something exceptionally comforting about this omen. It was a new day—for him and the company. The prospect of what was to come made his morning routine fly by as he made his way to the office where he would be spending the next eight hours in a deep huddle with his *new* team.

Jacob made sure to get in early to set up the conference room. He brought in trays with bagels and cream cheese, bottles of orange juice, and other healthy snacks to keep them all well fed and physically energized for the upcoming eight-hour kick-off meeting. He made sure there were plenty of water bottles for everyone, as well as containers full of Starbucks coffee to keep everyone awake, in the zone, and ready to strategize their new path.

As the team began to assemble, this meeting was already different from the previous ones that had taken place in this same room. Those meetings were always met with dread and worry about what message (usually a negative one) would be shared. Today, the window blinds were open to let the sun shine brightly into the room. The team began to arrive and settle in, pleasantly surprised by the food and drinks spread before them.

Andy, Jacki, and Jamie were all very excited to be part of the strategy meeting that would set the course for the company. They knew that Jacob's heart was in the right place, but he needed some guidance. They knew that Sam was the perfect person to help focus Jacob and facilitate the team in creating a new, actionable plan to reconnect with the fundamentals of the company and its growth.

Jacob knew he had the right people at the table to blaze the trail of growth for the company. It felt so great to have gotten rid of the toxic people in the organization.

The clock read 7:45 a.m. and Sam walked in. They all shook hands, shared some laughs about last night's ballgame, caught up on some small talk, and were ready to go by 8:00 a.m. sharp. The conference room was outfitted with a whiteboard and a fresh set of markers to help get the conversations going.

Sam handed out packets containing high-level strategy worksheets that would be used throughout the following week. He asked everyone to set these aside as it would be some time before they would begin using them, and a lot needed to be learned and accomplished before they could be cracked open.

He began the meeting by asking everyone what he or she wanted to accomplish. Everyone went around the room and answered. This gave Sam a deep understanding of what he needed to do to make sure everyone left the day feeling fulfilled. He was also focusing on their pressing issues, making sure that they were not only addressed, but that solutions with an action plan to achieve them would be provided by the end of the day.

Sam kicked off the meeting saying, "Okay, team, now that we know what we want to accomplish, let's dive in."

The leadership team was ready to get started. Jacob had his Expo markers in his right hand and the whiteboard behind him—ready to write and create and build.

"Team," Jacob said, "I want to welcome everyone today. Today, we are going to begin creating the new roadmap for TBM. Before we really dive in, I want everyone to take five minutes and answer any emails or any follow-up work that is on your mind. Then we will get started. I don't want any distractions."

The team was appreciative of the five minute "clearing period" Jacob had suggested. And, it gave Jacob a moment to send Joanna a quick text. They all took care of their last-minute distractions, put their phones away, then took to their notebooks and pens.

The excitement in the room was almost palpable. These people were excited to get started! This was one of the things that gave Sam a rush in his business. He loved the moment when the team was getting started on the rebirth of the company. The clean-up meetings always excited people but left most of them nervous. Once Sam could get his arms wrapped around the company, the dramatic and impactful changes would begin. That usually began to happen on the day when leadership roadmap blueprinting started. The team took obvious notice of Sam's excitement, which again assured them that they were in the right hands to grow the company they cared about. The same company that was currently stuck and off track.

Sam began, "Team, before we get started, we need to clean up something that is very evident in the organization: everyone needs clarity on what his or her role and responsibility is within the organization. There are too many people doing the same things, repeating the same tasks, and there is a breakdown in communication within the company walls when this happens. So, to get started, let's make an organizational chart on the board. Our next activity is to discuss, define, and document each person's role and responsibility. Then, we'll tackle creating a plan for rolling it all out."

Sam then wrote out all of the necessary spots in the organizational chart, with input from the team. He wrote everyone's name and left enough room under each person's name to write three to five bullet points about what each person should be doing. He then put a line under each person's name to define their unique superpower. What was the *one* thing this person excelled at and what was their unique power within the company walls? This was the first task the team was asked to accomplish in the meeting.

Sam began to set the pace of the meeting, starting with the organizational chart. He began instructing the team.

"Now is the time to clean up the foundation of the entire company. When I see problems in a company, it is typical for those problems to stem from a lack in the fundamental understanding of the basics. Who does what? Why do they do what they do, and how do they accomplish what they do? It is so vitally important that everyone in the organization understands what everyone else does. At a minimum, everyone must possess a basic understanding of the organizational chart. This helps in many ways, but let's list a few important ones:

- It prevents the doubling of work by multiple people.

- No ambiguity: everyone knows who to go to when that certain 'something' needs to get done.
- It speeds along the decision-making process because everyone knows who to go to for 'result decision making' the first time. What does this mean? No need to go to everyone in the company before you find the one person you needed in the first place. This gets the decision made faster, keeping the assembly line moving efficiently and smoothly and allowing people to get to their next task quickly.
- It reduces errors because it makes everyone somewhat of an expert in their skillset and gets an idea of all the potential obstacles that may come their way. If they don't know the answer, they have enough past trend reports in their heads or on paper to actually *make* a decision for the needed party."

He continued, "The most critical thing this does, which is going to sound very childish, but I didn't make the rules, and it is a part of human nature: when people in the company see that you are in 'closed door meetings' with certain people they *always* want to know what is going on and what you were talking about. If they knew what that person's role and responsibility are, they would more often than not assume you were talking about what they are doing and how to evolve their own role, themselves, or their department. When the 'behind closed doors' culture exists, it is *very* toxic to the culture of the company. So from now on, transparency is the name of the game."

Jamie, Jacki, and Andy all began smirking when Sam started talking about this, fixing their gazes in Jacob's direction until Jacob eventually spoke.

"Sam, I'm guilty of this. I hear all the time that people think I'm having all these '*secret* behind closed doors' meetings, which was never my intention. I just, typically like my privacy and don't want to disrupt people when I'm meeting with others. I need to be able to speak as freely as I need to at that moment. I want everyone to be able to speak freely as well, so we can think of ideas and grow the company."

"Jacob, I hear you. It's innocent ninety percent of the time, and most leaders or business owners don't realize the negative ramifications that these types of meetings can have on a company. Typically, this happens when people don't see action or growth resulting from those meetings. I am going to give you a quick fix for that one, but first tell me this, everyone: on a scale from one to ten, with ten being the extreme, how big of an issue do you all think this is?"

The question was an honest one, and no one jumped to answer. Each deliberated silently and eventually they went around the table to discuss their answer. Their answers averaged at roughly an eight.

"Okay, here is a quick fix, Jacob. Remind me, do you have weekly staff meetings?"

"Yes, Sam, we have them every Tuesday morning," Jacob answered.

"Do you have the division heads, Andy, Jamie, and Jacki, report at those meetings?" Sam questioned.

"Sometimes I do, Sam, but not all the time," Jacob said.

"I want them to be a staple at those meetings. Each week they need to speak, and each week they need to talk about what they discussed with you at your meetings with their departments. Always end with a high-level review of what you are doing and, most importantly, what those action items and deadlines are. They don't always have to be concrete, but they need to see that they are going to see and experience change. The change is more transparency from you, Jacob, to your entire company. Once they see this, they will begin to trust you more. You need to set the stage for what is about to come, so they can see you working on their behalf, and can get physically and emotionally invested.

"The thing that throws employees off is when you drop a bomb on them full of information and changes. They need to feel as if they are in the loop so they can understand the information given and that their contribution to the company matters. One of the main responsibilities of the company leaders is to keep the company in motion and make sure everyone feels like they are appreciated and that they matter. You will begin to see a shift and a change in your people when you do this."

Andy cut in, "Sam, thanks. That was powerful information. It sounds like you just gave us a simple tool that will make a huge impact around here. I, for one, am excited to put that in motion, as you would say," he joked. Everyone laughed and was just as excited to experiment with the best practice that Sam just gave them. They hoped it would work just as Sam predicted.

"Okay, team, now let's write everyone on the board. I'm going to leave a blank line next to each name and a space under the name so we can write out the role and responsibility belonging to each person, along with their unique ability," Sam continued. He motioned for Jacob to begin adding the names to the whiteboard, just as he had instructed.

"Sam, can you explain what a unique superpower is again?" Jamie asked, knowing that everyone was wondering the same thing. Sam smirked, as a teacher might when he knows students are on the edge of their seats.

"Sure, Jamie, absolutely I can. Your unique superpower is that special gift or talent. Everyone's got one. It is the *one* thing that you excel at. That you're above-average at. Something you do better than the next person. What do you think your unique ability is, Jamie?"

"Wow, Sam, I never thought about it," she said, as she looked down at her notepad, a bit embarrassed for not being able to answer the question. She then looked up towards Jacob standing at the whiteboard. He nodded with a smile of encouragement, letting her know that it was okay that she was not sure yet. They smiled at each other. She would be sure very soon. Sam spoke again, to help her out.

"Most people don't. Team, what is Jamie's unique superpower in the company?"

"Jamie, I think your unique superpower is seeing what most people don't see. You have a gift that is to see the abstract and turn it into something obvious and awesome. That is why you are so good at marketing; you can see what others can't and create a campaign that makes people pay attention and think, 'Wow, why haven't I thought of that before?'" Andy answered.

"Thanks, Andy, I appreciate that. I think you are right. I never really thought about it as my unique superpower. It's just what I love to do. I don't even feel like I have to work at it," she responded.

"Exactly! That is when you know you are in your unique superpower. It doesn't feel like work. It comes out so naturally that it's like a gift from above. Other people have described it to me as euphoric: it's an understanding of how to do or explain something that they may have little training in and *boom!* It just talks to them and oozes right out of them. If you are aware enough, then you turn that into your career. It's where true passion comes from," Sam said, tapping into his own superpower.

Jacki sat quietly, with a curious look on her face. Sam asked her to share what she was thinking.

"Sam, that was amazing just to listen to. I can't stop thinking about what my unique superpower is."

Chuckling and excited, Sam responded to her enthusiasm by saying, "We are going to talk about yours and everyone's. Once you know everyone's role and responsibility and his or her unique superpower, the communication in the company hits the next level because everyone begins to understand each other in a new way."

They were all eating out of his hand now. Jacob walked to the back counter and poured himself a cup of coffee. He watched the steam rise from the top as he brought it toward his lips. He couldn't help but smile. Four other people in this room were just shot through the roof with excitement. They were excited to help him build his company. They were *excited!* That felt damn good. And it was something he hadn't felt in months, maybe even years.

The team spent the next two and a half hours writing out the roles and responsibilities of each person in the company, together with their unique superpower.

Almost visibly, the light bulbs were flipping on in each person's mind, and they could see how managing the people in this company was going to become much more doable. They had gained a deeper understanding of who each person was. People and roles were even exchanged for a better fit, one that made more sense for the organization. They were so excited to share everything with the other employees.

"Great job, everyone," Sam said. "I know you're excited, but let's take a ten-minute break. Next, we need to dive into everyone's driver."

"Driver? What's that?" Jacob asked.

"I'll tell you after our ten-minute break," Sam said and smiled at Jacob.

* * * *

As the clock counted down that ten-minute break, there was no distracting the team. Each of them sat anxiously waiting to resume the meeting and learn what this driver was all about. They refilled their coffee cups and piled their plates. It was time to learn more. Andy did not hesitate to speak immediately.

"Sam, what is someone's 'driver?'" he said in a humorous sort of way. "Do you mean they need to play golf or drive a Tesla?" Everyone laughed.

Andy Monterey was as solid as they came and Jacob knew he couldn't build his business without him. Well, he could, but not as quickly. He knew that, in time, Andy would become a partner in the company. That was an insight that Sam later shared with Jacob in a private one-on-one, as well. That validation was enough proof and foreshadowing that Jacob knew a plan had to be put in place for this to happen sooner rather than later. He was one of the hardest-working people Jacob had ever worked with. Sam could sense the same thing having known Andy only for a few days.

He was not your typical salesperson. He never graduated from college, but his street sense and ability to read people surpassed that of any Ivy League graduate. You could not teach the skills Andy possessed, they were natural talents. His drive, ambition, and ability to connect with people—whether clients or people he managed—was mesmerizing.

Jacob had made Andy the new head of sales and he was very excited to take on the role. He had managed people in his past career and knew the ins-and-outs of empowering his team without micromanaging them. He grew up with little means, even though his father was a wealthy doctor. They were a family that did not spend frivolously and wanted their children to understand the value of a dollar. His father gave him the foundation and discipline to fight hard for what he wanted and the acumen to grow a strong business, just as his father built his successful medical practice.

Andy was a bit rough around the edges, with very little filter; but, yet, he knew how to throw out a joke and get the crowd laughing. He was even doing it today in the conference room! Nothing was off limits for him. If you did something that was off or odd, Andy would pick up on it and never let you forget it. He was one of those people who seemed to get away with everything. He kind of resembled a cross between Rodney Dangerfield and Mark Zuckerberg, with big ears and a big nose on a six-foot, two-inch frame.

Sam was the first to respond to Andy's quip. "No, Andy, that is not the type of driver I am talking about. We're talking about the reason each one of us—that includes you—gets out of bed in the morning.

"What is the one thing, maybe two, that ignites people to do their best every day? It is what speaks to their soul and is their personal mission in life. These drivers are usually good, healthy drivers that push them to succeed, but sometimes there can be unhealthy drivers, too. Those are typically very deeply rooted in a person's DNA.

"You're not going to be able to change the driver; but, in order to be successful, you have to figure out your own driver, and your people's drivers, and how to manage all of them. The trick is to manage the driver without the person ever knowing you are doing it. If you are doing it right, they will think and say things like 'Wow, they really know me and get me.'

"Why don't you want people to know that you are guiding them through their driver? Simple. If they know it, then it seems contrived, less personal. Many times people don't know what their own drivers are. On the surface, they will say they are driven by money. But, if you really listen and get to know your team, you will understand what keeps them up at night and gets them up in the morning ready to conquer the world and their business.

"Many people will say they are driven by money, but that is never the driving force. For example, the driving force may be that they grew up on food stamps and are determined to never have that situation for their children. It is different for every person," Sam finished.

The team's gaze was locked on Sam. The morning session had inspired them to understand the changes that were coming to TBM, but this, this was different. Now he was getting a read on each of them, and they knew it, and they liked it.

Jacob broke the silence, "Wow, Sam, that seems really difficult. As I think about everyone on my team, I don't know if I have ever thought about anything like that. If I'm being completely honest, I am always managing people the way I think and asking them or getting them to do things on my timeframe, based on *my* immediate needs." He paused, took a sip of coffee, then continued, "I have never even thought about what may be driving them to get things accomplished. That being said, I have always done my best to be a team player and to be kind to my team. But, it has always been about *my* daily driver to get things done with urgency. When I think about it, if I had understood their drivers, along with the roles and responsibilities, and their superpowers that we talked about before, my conversations with my team—or anyone for that matter —would be completely different and more them-centric and not so me-centric."

Jamie, Andy, and Jacki all nodded their heads in agreement. This was a perspective they had never been given before. They could feel how positively impacted the company would be if these ideas were implemented on a daily basis. It would work for the growth of the business, and for each individual's growth, as well.

"Jacob, you are on the right path in your thinking. When you have the foundational understanding of all this, it begins to shift your company's culture in an extraordinary way. You will begin to see your people, not only more connected to each of you individually and as a leadership team, but to the company as a whole. You are creating a deeper loyalty to the company as you continue to improve your understanding of your people and offer them an environment where they feel heard and appreciated. That actually makes them feel like they matter, and it begins to increase their trust in you and the organization," Sam said.

Jacki cut in, "Sam, I can really see how these shifts in thinking will change so much in the company. Basically, you are helping us discover a new mindset for growing ourselves and this business."

Each person around the table found themselves again nodding in agreement, and they all had an optimistic smile creeping onto their faces.

"Jacki, well said. You get it," Sam affirmed.

Everyone took a deep breath and fell back into their chairs. The discussion brought to mind many situations that could have played out differently over the last few months, with a more productive outcome. If only they had known about these tools sooner! Sam was constantly reminding them that all of their old methods—the tools, mindset, and best practices—got them to where they are today. And that's something. These new tools were going to get them where they wanted to be *next*.

There was no point in looking back with regret, Sam reminded them. It's just too easy to judge in hindsight. Over and over, he repeated that they could not change the way they did things in the past. But, moving forward, they had the power to effect positive change: the power to work smarter and be more effective. He encouraged them to stay present and enjoy the benefits of what he was teaching them.

The team spent the next hour brainstorming. They discussed each employee and identified their drivers. Sam facilitated the conversation until it was fully exhausted.

They now had a proper organizational chart, complete with roles and responsibilities, identified unique superpowers, and listed drivers. They felt accomplished and grateful for this experience with Sam. He was truly transforming everyone's mindset, which was clearly translating into a transformation in the business. As they gazed around the room, each one of them was thinking the same thing: *How are we going to implement all of this into our day-to-day operations?*

Sam saw their expressions. As though reading minds, he said, "Team, I know what you are all thinking and feeling right now. You're asking yourself, 'How do we implement this?' Am I right?"

Everyone nodded. Almost in unison, everyone asked, "How do we make this part of our day as we walk and talk with our people?"

"Well, folks," Sam began, "here comes the challenging part: implementing everything we just talked about along with the other critical fundamentals we will explore next.

"The critical item that everyone absolutely must understand is this: as we look at the leadership team in this room, we have four very talented people. That being said, you all need a deeper understanding of each other and the roles you play in making everything happen. It's very simple when you think about it.

"Jacob, you are a visionary, and you need to always maintain the vision of the company, together with each employee's personal vision of how they want to grow within the company. It is your responsibility to make sure you inspire and influence this company to follow your leadership and buy into your vision.

"Andy, as the leader of the sales group, you need to hold the sales vision and the standards that your team will be expected to achieve. You will also ensure that each salesperson is doing what they say they are going to do *and* that they are executing the challenges you set for them to grow their business, as well. You need to make sure that you implement and integrate the daily messages that you and the leadership want to be communicated to the sales department. As you manage them, you need to guide them to the growth that the company needs, but also the growth they desire. You are their biggest cheerleader, but you are also their coach who pushes them outside their comfort zone.

"Jacki, your role is to make sure that everything gets implemented and integrated into the company. Since you run the office, you need to make sure that the vision and sales goals have a constant flow of motion and implementation for the salespeople. Some days, you may feel like all you are doing is reminding people to do what they said they were going to do, pushing paper and emails all day."

"That is exactly how I feel many days as it is!" she exclaimed.

"Jacki, don't underestimate the power and importance of that role. It is critical, and you are the right person to be in that role. There will be plenty of times when you will feel like you can't measure what you do every day. But, the long-term measurable results will be there. I promise," he assured her.

"Thanks for saying that, Sam. Sometimes, I feel like I am annoying other team members and that I am not as valuable as some of the others because I am doing exactly what you just said. I watch the other leadership team do things they can measure. Then, here I am pushing people, arranging workshops, nagging them to do what they said they were going to do, getting them this, getting them that…"

Jacob chimed in, "Jacki, I'm really glad you brought that up because I want to tell you right now that you are just as important to the company as the rest of us are. And, what you do, if it has gone unrecognized or unnoticed, I apologize. I apologize that I have not thanked you enough or given you the accolades you deserve. It just always seems like you've got it handled. All of it."

Andy and Jamie were both quick to agree with Jacob. They reassured Jacki and gave her the praise she deserved. They also now understood that they needed to do more of this, not only to recognize her effort but also to make sure that the whole company knew just how important she was to its success.

Sam continued, "Jamie, your role is something of a combination of visionary and implementer. Because you are marketing this company and this brand, we want to make sure that you have the creative freedom to have a vision and then work with your team to implement that vision. It's important to understand these high-level roles you play because you are more of a leader than you think. Everything you do and say is examined under a microscope. You need to understand and own these visionary and implementer roles of yours. You get to make things happen and keep things in action mode. When you fully understand and own it, your leadership and influence will begin to grow to new heights.

"So, if you say you are going to do something and you don't, or your people don't see action, you are dramatically hurting yourself, the leadership team, and the culture of your company. The reason for this is this: you are the keepers of the vision, and you make sure things are getting implemented. If you don't do what you say you are going to do, when you say you are doing to do it, no one will. Leadership is then missing, and things begin to go downhill. In many cases, the leadership team doesn't even realize it's happening and then the notion that the leadership team is an exception to their own rules becomes a nasty undercurrent of the company. You all need to commit that this will not happen. You must own it. Everyone in?"

Unanimously, they said, "Yes, we're in."

"Okay, then, repeat after me: 'As a leader, visionary, and implementer I must always do what I say I am going to do, when I say I am going to do it.'"

They all repeated after him.

Sam continued, "I want to give you a tool for everyday use. Walk and talk among your people, every day. Mix business and personal, so you are able to get feedback on what's important to them and to yourself. So everyone can experience movement and growth individually and for the company as a whole."

As the day was winding to a close, Sam said, "Okay, team, next week we will kick off this transformation and first on our agenda is to jump into the DNA of the company and talk about why you do what you do: your root values, your focus, your purpose, your niche in the company. We'll also talk about your ideal client and your company message. But, we've reached the end of the day now, so go home and get some rest. We'll start on that first thing Monday morning. But here's what I need from you tomorrow and Friday. If you need to come in early or stay late, do so. Take care of any business that you need to take care of, because next week, for five days, I need your full attention."

* * * *

This had been an intense—but incredibly rewarding—day of coaching. As Jacob walked to his car, he dialed Dr. Marc's number and impatiently waited through each ring. He couldn't wait to thank Dr. Marc and tell him what he had just been through. After three rings, Dr. Marc answered the phone.

"Dr. Marc, it's Jacob. How are you?" Jacob said.

"Hey, Jacob!" Dr. Marc said joyfully, "How are you, kiddo?"

"I'm doing great! We finished our introductory leadership meeting with Sam, and I just wanted to call and thank you for connecting me with him. Everything is going better than I could have imagined! Sam is really opening our eyes to a brand-new mindset, and I am really grateful to him, to you, and to everyone who got me to this place I'm in today."

"Jacob, you've just made my day. I couldn't be happier for you. I knew he would be a perfect fit for you and the company. Sam just has a way about him that makes everything seem simple, almost obvious, doesn't he, Jacob?" Dr. Marc asked.

"He sure does, Dr. Marc! Everything he said seems exactly that: simple and obvious. I find myself thinking, *How did I not do any of this years ago*? I have read a lot about what he is talking about. I've seen it in other companies. I've heard it talked about in seminars for years; yet, Sam comes in and just lays it all out as easy as 1-2-3," Jacob said, overly confident in the new process. Dr. Marc and Jacob both shared a laugh.

"Jacob, Sam has a gift for making the complicated seem simple. When you are with him, he is able to advise you so that all the minutiae and distractions floating around in your head can just disappear. You know, so you can focus on what you have been talking about for years," Dr. Marc summarized.

"Exactly."

"Jacob, you know I think the world of Sam. He is a master facilitator and will help you retool your company's systems, processes, and mindset. I know he will. But, I want you to remember something: you need to always commit to taking some quiet, executive time to yourself. Maybe something like thirty minutes a week. You will accelerate your work with him by taking your own executive time," Dr. Marc said.

"I hear you, Dr. Marc. You always seem to have the perfect thing to say when we talk," Jacob noticed.

"Thanks, Jacob, I do my best," he said, laughing. "Now, I'm heading into a doctor's appointment and have to run, but please keep me in the loop. I know you are busy with Sam and retooling your business right now, but let's grab lunch sometime soon. Email me some dates that work for you. I'm off on Wednesdays."

"Will do, Dr. Marc. I'll get that out to you in the next couple days," Jacob said, excited to catch up with Dr. Marc.

"Sounds great. Please give Sam my regards."

"You got it, Dr. Marc. Thanks again," Jacob confirmed.

"You're welcome," replied the dentist, "and you can stop thanking me so much!"

* * * *

Jacob noticed over the next couple of days that the team was busily trying to get everything done in preparation for Sam's arrival on Monday. He too was taking Sam's challenge to give him his full attention. Thursday and Friday flew by; everything was set for their coach's arrival.

On Monday, the team gathered in the conference room with Sam, who wasted no time kicking off the meeting. He started in right away, "Alright, team," Sam said excitedly, "we are going to talk about the DNA of your company. What is this? The DNA is clear messaging about key elements of your business:

- Mission Statement
- Vision
- Values
- Focus
- Niche in the Marketplace
- Defining Your Ideal Clients
- Company Standards
- Culture

- Customer Service Standards
- And, of course, Your Purpose

Do you have any of this in writing right now?" he asked in Jacob's direction.

"No, we don't," Jacob replied as he began scribbling on the pad of paper in front of him. "I know this sounds crazy, but it always just seemed like we had all of that. But, when you stop and ask, the answer is no. I'm embarrassed to even say this because it seems so fundamental. *How could we NOT have that*?" He stopped for a second to gather himself, a bit frustrated at his lack of leadership in this regard.

He continued, "My intention was to do it when I started the company, but one thing led to another, then the deals started coming in, and we started hiring to meet the needs of the company's growth and ..."

Sam interrupted him and asked, "Have you ever had a recruiting business plan, Jacob?"

"No, and it's beginning to seem like I never had any real plan to begin with." The joys of Wednesday's victories seemed to be a distant memory. This was a new day, and so far it wasn't going well. Frustration was coming at him like a runaway freight train.

Sam saw this scenario over and over again in the thousands of companies he had worked with over the years. Companies were operating by the seat of their pants with one major flaw in common: no planning! Sam just could not comprehend this way of operating.

Sam was always a planner. He also loved sports, like most of his clients did. Everyone understood that in business, like sports, you have to practice and plan to win on game day. You cannot just show up and think you are going to win the game without some effort beforehand. Yet, he found that most business people never took the time to map out a strategy. They operated reactively instead of proactively in how they ran their businesses. It was, in fact, a key nuance that distinguished low to moderate growth as compared to big-time growth.

Planning. That's it. The businesses that did the most consistent and most effective planning grew the most and the fastest. Just like the old advice that you'll end up buying way too much if you go grocery shopping without a list. Planning is the ultimate secret to success and thinking big.

Sam began his instruction by asking, "Andy, Jacki, and Jamie: How do you feel about the company not having a plan in place? How do the people you manage feel about the company not having a plan in place?"

215

They went around the room, and the overall response was clear; they all felt unsettled. The company felt unsettled, and so did the employees.

"Now that you know that your team from top to bottom feels unsettled, do you understand the importance of clearly defining the DNA—the foundation—of your company? If people are going to come to work every day, bringing their best selves—their commitment, their energy, and their drive—they need to understand for whom they are doing it and why they are doing it. They need to understand the guts of the organization and what this company stands for." Sam looked firmly at Jacob for the response.

Jacob answered quietly, but truthfully, "Sam, I get it. I'm on board. I feel like I fucked up and I hear you. You are absolutely right."

"Jacob, I don't want you to get negative about this, I just want to make sure that as the owner of this company you understand the importance of this and that you *own* it. If you don't, *no one* will," Sam said soothingly as he saw Jacob teetering on the edge of frustration, poised to jump.

Jacob gazed at his leadership team and said empathically, "Jacki, Jamie, Andy: I am committed to creating this roadmap with you and owning it with the most energy I have ever given to anything in my life. I can and will lead by example, and I will live it. You have my word. And I need to know that you will do the same." They all individually smiled and gave Jacob their word that they were in it to win it and that they most definitely would also own it.

As the reality of those words soaked in, Sam spoke up, "Okay, team, let's talk about what each of these means:

- Your Mission Statement - A sentence or two that defines who and what you are.
- Your Vision - Where you are going and how you will get there.
- Your Values - The principles and standards that define the company.
- Your Focus - What do you sell? What is your product? What are its benefits?
- Niche in the Marketplace - What is unique about you?
- Defining Your Ideal Clients - Who are they and why do they buy your product? What is their pain? How are you the solution? How are you messaging this?
- Standards - The bar to which you have set yourselves and your company.
- Customer Service Standards - The experience and level of service your client will have by working with you and choosing your services and products.

- Culture - The vibe of your internal culture and what clients and employees experience and feel the moment they walk through your door.
- Your Purpose - The intention of what you stand for and want to become."

The clarifications Sam gave helped the team to have an in-depth meeting. Time seemed to fly, but really it was just a couple of hours. They discussed all the departments, people, and competitors, and then mixed it together with what was working and what was not working within the company walls. They took the good, left the bad, and created clarity where it was lacking. They constructed a new and improved company DNA. Sam helped them put something powerful on paper that began really shaping both their company and their people in the direction they had hoped. They knew they had been stuck. Now they knew why.

As they continued to work with Sam, it became clear that they needed to begin having the mindset of not only doing things differently but also investing in themselves and the company to ensure that someone like Sam would guide them to their next level. It was abundantly clear that they could never have done this on their own without him—or someone like him—facilitating, engaging, and pushing them to dig deep below the surface and find honest, real answers.

Throughout the day, they were in their team meeting with intense moments of direct conversations as Sam pushed them to establish their thoughts and provide clarity in their responses. Sam kept reminding them throughout the day, "If you are unclear and can't get below the surface, your people never will. You need to build and train your muscle so you can push and train theirs. That is your responsibility as a leader."

He would also remind them, "No one wants to be complacent. People need to be pushed based on their role and responsibility, using their unique superpower and their driver, when they are the right person who buys into the DNA of the firm. Your people need YOU to help them grow and take them to their next level."

Sam expected only the best from those in the room. What they did not realize was that he was retraining them to retrain their people. They had never experienced this type of push before. Sam had a way of getting people to open up and talk without raising his voice and without being judgmental. He was always fair but never accepted *I don't know,* or *I can't do this*. There was always a way to dig deeper, and Sam was a master at finding it. Seeing alternate perspectives was one of his fortes, and so was engaging others to see those perspectives. In those moments, everyone experienced a change in the making.

Sam was giving them a gift, which they would only come to truly appreciate once they began it.

It was a long, productive day. The team was spent, and thankfully Sam called the dynamic strategy day officially done. He gave his closing remarks for the day, recapping the day's lessons, and left with a riddle before they were to see each other the next day, punctually at 8:00 a.m.

Before dismissing them for the day, he riddled, "Five frogs are sitting on a log. Four decide to jump off. How many frogs are left on the log?"

He asked each of them to write down their answer and then called them, one by one, to reveal their response. They were all suspicious that the answer was not as obvious as it seemed. All but one got it wrong.

Sam continued, "Today was a great day of transformation—a metamorphosis if you will. You all worked very hard to do what needed to get done, and I appreciate all of your efforts, and you all should appreciate each other for what was created in this room today. You will look back years from now and remember how you reset and recharged the company today. That's huge! The key to everything we talked about is *action*. You must all create *action* in the company and create a constant flow of motion, so action is always in process. Do you agree?"

"Yes, Sam, we agree," they all answered light-heartedly.

"Okay, good. Since you all agree, I'll give you the answer to the riddle. The answer is five."

Everyone in the room shouted, "I knew it!" Even the ones who were wrong.

"Does anyone know why it's five?"

Jamie was the first to speak up, "I know, Sam. Because the four frogs had only decided to jump, they never did. They didn't take *action*!"

"Correct, Jamie. They didn't take action. We all decided to do some pretty amazing things today. Now, it is time to take action. Without action, nothing works," Sam responded. "Do you want to know how to take action for turbo-charged growth?"

In near-perfect unison, they all exclaimed, "Yes! Sam, of course we do."

"Great. Then hold yourselves accountable and, more importantly, be open to holding each other accountable. Don't get mad when someone calls you out that you didn't do what you said you were going to do. Be open for the feedback and accountability that you need to be strong and effective.

"If you, as leaders of the company, hold each other accountable, you will lead by example. Your people see not what you say, but what you do. Remember this, and remember it forever: It is not what you preach, it is what you tolerate. What you preach and tolerate … when it comes to yourselves, each other, and your company. Let that be a mantra for how you not only run this business but your lives, as well."

"Sam, how do you always know how to layer in such a great life lesson when you are talking business? It's so refreshing and inspiring!" Jamie asked with a smile.

Sam always had a way of tying in life lessons while delivering a business lesson. They were always at the perfect time—as if scripted that way. It was effortless for him.

"Jamie, what I hope you are picking up on—and what I am doing my best to teach you—is that when you wait for the right opportunity to do and say the right thing, you build trust and begin to get the best out of each other, and the people you manage. We will talk more about that later. In the meantime, is everyone into owning action?"

"Yes, Sam, we are in. We will own action." The team cheered, thanking Sam for an incredible day. After shaking hands, they returned to their desks to finish some follow-up work that would make them prepared to take on the next day with Sam.

"Hey, Sam, before we leave, what are we talking about tomorrow?" Jacki asked.

"Well, I wouldn't want to ruin the surprise, and I don't want you overthinking things in advance. I need your rawness in the room," Sam answered, laughingly.

"Deal!" Jacki said as she smiled and shut the door behind her. Sam was left in the conference room alone, very proud of the team and the work they just accomplished. Tomorrow was going to be even more exciting than today. He could not wait to tackle the new issues with this team.

As he zipped up the Tumi backpack he'd been hauling around for years, he felt accomplished. Sam looked forward to this feeling—of helping people to become better versions of themselves, not to mention the side benefit of watching them grow their businesses because of it. He loved being able to give his clients tools that seemed so obvious and so natural to him. These tools helped people get unstuck and onto the path of growth, both professionally and personally. Sam ended the day feeling fulfilled by this, his own driver.

Chapter 18: The Business Plan

Timing, perseverance, and ten years of trying will eventually make you look like an overnight success.
- Biz Stone, Twitter co-founder

The Tuesday morning drive was wet due to rain, but that didn't deter anyone from arriving at the conference room table early. Breakfast from the bakery down the street was already invitingly laid out. Always homemade, fresh, and full of natural ingredients, it was totally a crowd favorite. Carafes of the bakery's secret recipe coffee accompanied the delicious food.

Jamie, however, was notorious for always showing up late with her grande, non-fat, half-caf-half-decaf, coconut milk with two sugars in the raw from Starbucks. They all poked fun at her because of how embarrassing it was to be with her when she ordered it. But, it started her day with a smile, and she always brought that smile into the office, on good days and bad.

Sam arrived at the office twenty minutes before everyone else and enjoyed talking to the employees as they arrived, as well as the delivery kid from the bakery. Sam always loved talking to working people. It didn't matter if they were making deliveries, baristas, sandwich makers, janitors, or CEOs of the smallest companies. Sam loved talking to everyone equally because everyone had a story and he loved to hear them. He was always curious and asked really great questions that made people feel like he was really interested in them. That's because he was. This is what kept Sam's finger on the pulse of what his clients—or prospective clients—in any market or industry wanted to know.

Sam always knew what people were thinking, and he could morph that knowledge into changing companies for the better. He never revealed his client roster because he held their confidence in such high regard. Sam said the same thing to all of his clients, "I'll never tell anyone I work with you but feel free to tell everyone that you work with me." They all got a good laugh out of it, but this was how Sam was able to grow his own business. His clients were located throughout the world and would consistently refer him to others.

Normally not a coffee drinker, today Sam was trying this famous coffee from everyone's favorite bakery. He welcomed each team member into the conference room with a firm handshake, their eyes meeting, and asking how they were today. He looked them in the eyes, particularly because that is how he greeted people, especially clients, but also because it helped him to get a read of each individual and see how they were landing after yesterday's strategy session.

Sam had a way of reading people. He could interpret body language and sense what they were thinking. He could determine what they were upset about, or what they had on their minds. He was a master at bringing all of it out on the table and working through it until it was resolved, getting rid of the angst and issues. No one was safe when Sam called out angst in the room. He had two rules, which he announced yesterday before the meeting started.

1. "It may get a bit rough in the room at times, but I promise you, I will make sure everything gets cleaned up and back in order before we end the day."

Not much had come up the first day, but Sam anticipated more of this type of facilitating on day two. He could just sense it. The team was more comfortable, with a new level of thinking and would now be in a position to be a bit more vulnerable and speak the truth, give honest opinions, and directly indicate what they have been seeing when things were being done the "wrong" way. Sam was looking forward to this next level of leadership communication because this would be where the real magic happened.

2. Sam started each meeting with a business clearing. Everyone had five minutes to clear up anything they had on their mind. If they needed to answer a quick email, send an email or follow up with a client or team member, this was

their time to do so. It didn't matter *what* they needed to clear; it just mattered that it was done *now*. Sam gave everyone five minutes to clear up their outstanding matters and then their phones and tablets had to be put away until the next break.

"Okay, team. Everybody ready?" Sam asked.

The team enthusiastically responded all at once, "Ready, Sam!"

"One of the first things I asked of Jacob was to see the company's business plan, as well as the business plans for the department heads. Does anyone want to guess what Jacob told me?" Sam began their meeting.

"I know exactly what he told you. He told you we don't have one. We just talked about doing one," Jacki answered.

"And, how is that working for you and your team?" Sam continued to ask.

"Not well. Nothing runs like it should. My father's father worked at Ford Motor Company and always preached the importance of an assembly line," Jacki said.

"Jacki, you're right on. Tell me more. I talk about that, too, with my clients, but I want to hear what your grandpa used to say."

"Well, he said it was the ultimate system. Everything was methodical, and everyone knew what everyone else was supposed to do. If one part of the line was off, everything was off. My grandfather ran his life with that type of thinking and tried to instill that philosophy in all of us."

"That must be why you are so organized and have been pushing for this type of meeting for the past couple years, Jacki," realized Jacob aloud. "I'm sorry it took me so long to listen and take action on what now in hindsight seems so much more important than it did. Thank you, Jacki, for pushing this," Jacob said to her.

"Hey," Jacki said jokingly, "I'm good like that." She shrugged her shoulders in a sarcastic yet coolly confident way.

"Jacki, that is a great synopsis of an assembly line. Your grandpa was a wise man. Your business plans are the structure, order, and plan of the assembly line that is your business. By the time we leave today, each of you will be operating from a company business plan as well as a department business plan. You will have business plans for your people and, where appropriate, you will work with them to create their own business plan for the year. Understand?" Sam said.

"Sounds good," said the team. They mockingly rolled their eyes for added effect, in keeping with the jovial camaraderie Sam had begun.

Sam's goal was to showcase the effect of increased collaboration. Even small doses of sticking together build a more collaborative and fun environment. It is the little things, like this, that Sam knew kept a company's most important assets (the employees) coming back each and every day.

This would be a constant message for Jacob and his company, as it is for all companies that Sam worked with, and an ongoing message that persisted through the years. It's easy for everyone to get so busy that they forget this. So, Sam always brought back some quick-fix basics to jump-start the company's culture. Healthy culture equals a healthy environment, which equates to employees going the extra mile and thinking outside the box both for the company, and for the client.

Less than twenty minutes had passed when Sam announced that he was ready to start helping the team build the company's business plan.

"Okay, team, here is what we are going to do: we are going to create a business plan today. I'm all about making things simple. No reason to over-complicate anything. Set course for the big picture and reverse-engineer back to today, while filling in all the details needed to create the ultimate result we want.

"First, let me go over the highlights of what we will build. We will build out action plans and specific steps for this:

- A ten-year dream plan
- A five-year business plan
- A three-year business plan
- A one-year business plan
- Breaking down your one-year business plan into a ninety-day plan
- Breaking down your ninety-day plan into a thirty-day plan
- Breaking down your thirty-day plan into a list of each person's daily tasks
- A review of every metric we will use to measure your success and trends
- Review and put together trends so we can project and forecast the company's future and revenues, along with profits and margins

- Year-over-year everything so we can also project and forecast the company's future and revenues, along with profits and margins
- A full personal and business S.W.O.T analysis. (This is where we review your and the company's strengths, weaknesses, opportunities, and threats.)
- The top two results we want to achieve in the next thirty days
- Your current market share and market share goal within the next thirty days to one year
- Your current mindshare and mindshare goal within the next thirty days to one year
- The one measurable for the company, each person, and each department."

"Wow, Sam," Jacob responded, "when I said I didn't have a business plan, I really meant that I didn't have a business plan. Even the business plan I had in my mind looked and sounded nothing like that. I mean, *nothing like that*! The more I listen to you, Sam, the more I realize why I was stuck. We had none of these fundamentals in place."

Everyone chimed in in agreement. It was obvious that no one in the room had the skill set to facilitate a meeting like this, nor did they have the expertise to walk each other through the steps needed to complete the company's "assembly line," which was essential for achieving the growth they were hungry for.

Jacob was thinking back again, as he had many times throughout this process, about how fortunate he felt that Aria introduced him to Dr. Marc and how it all led to this moment. Everything pointed back to that moment when he felt enough courage to tell Aria how things were *really* going in his company. Because of that, all of this incredible change was happening. Aria was a real life changer.

Whenever someone asked Jacob how things were going, his canned response was, "Great! Everything's great!" Whether it was actually going well or horribly, the answer was the same. The problem with this response is that you are never open to receiving advice and quality feedback for your own growth. Jacob was happy and felt fortunate to have had that fateful day when he was truthful with Aria. He sent himself a reminder to call her after the meetings with Sam were over, to thank her for everything.

* * * *

As the conversation progressed and moved forward, the team could not believe how quickly the time had passed. They had only completed half of their business planning. Everyone was participating as Sam facilitated continual conversation, pushing each of them as only he could. His goal was for them to dig below the surface and create something that was not only attainable but also outside of their comfort zone. They were creating something incredibly detailed, with deadlines, an outline of assigned tasks, and a solid action plan with measurables so that everyone could hold each other accountable to those tasks.

The team loved creating their ten-year dream plan, their five-year plan, the three-year and one-year plans. But, they were most grateful for the way Sam worked with them to narrow everything down to a thirty-day plan that would be updated for the coming month by the 25th. Sam continually preached the importance of planning. Everyone was on board and looking forward to a break.

Sam addressed them, "Team, how accomplished do you feel now that we created the foundation of the business plans?"

"I am so excited, I can't take it," Jamie said, and then continued, "I feel as if I just got rid of a thousand huge monkeys off my shoulders and gained total clarity. I understand the roadmap. I really get where we are going and how we are going to get there. Thank you so much!"

"Jamie, thank you for that feedback. But, remember this: a business plan is easy to put together, but difficult to execute. Every one of you must put forth the effort *every day* and do the hard work to bring the business plan to life," Sam reminded her. "Deal, everyone?"

"Deal," everyone agreed with a smile as they stood up to take their fifteen-minute break.

Sam could see that these people were ready to take on the new challenge they set for themselves in their new business plans. Sam could see that this was a company that had something special and would go on to do big things.

These people understood hard work, and everyone seemed to have a natural discipline that Sam often noticed lacking in other companies. He knew that the smiles on their faces would influence their teams and back up the fact that everything they were doing to grow the company was a great fit for everyone, and in their best interest. Because of the way they were owning every point, the employees under them would certainly know they had their backs. And when you have that, you have trust; and, when you have both, you have a company that thrives!

Sam stood in the conference room, smiling contentedly. He had done his magic and given the team a gift. In return, he received one right back. This was a feeling that never got old for him. He lived for it.

The break had now slipped by and the team re-assembled in the conference room. Sam grabbed his Expo markers and began right where they had left off. They dove back in to create more clarity and finalize their business planning with all the components he had outlined earlier in the day.

Sam began by drawing a line on the whiteboard. To the left of the line, he wrote the words "Today's Date." To the far right end of the line, he wrote the words "Big Picture" and a blank line for a date. He drew an arrow from Big Picture to the left pointing back to Today's Date. In the middle of the line right under it, he wrote the word "Details." Everyone sat in silence as Sam drew what he considered an epic masterpiece. But, to those in the room in that moment, it was just a line with a few words.

He then began to explain. "Okay, everyone, we are going to spend time continually digging into the business plans we mapped out earlier. In this part of the session, we are going to make sure we have complete clarity and complete understanding of the action needed to accomplish our goals.

"On the board is a visual that I want you to adopt in all of your strategy meetings. It lays out everything you want to say, accomplish, and take action on in one easy line. For each piece of the business plan we discuss, we are going to determine what the big picture is and the date we want to accomplish it by. We are then going to reverse-engineer to today's date and fill in all the details needed to hit our goal."

Jamie cut in, "The journey to the big picture, Sam. I love it."

"I'm glad we are on the same page, Jamie, though we always seem to be," he laughed.

Jacob yelled out, "Well, we know who your favorite is Sam." He nudged Andy on the elbow, and they all chuckled.

Sam replied with a wink, "You are all my favorites." It was a nice attempt at a recovery, but no one believed it.

Sam refocused the group, "Let's get back to the board, shall we? When we can see where we are today, and where we want to go, *and* take the time to write in all the details with action items and deadlines, it makes the path to get there manageable. It's never easy, but it is manageable. If it was easy, of course, everyone would do it.

"The executive time needed each week and on each project to do this is *critical* to long-term success and clarity. When you get in this habit, you can begin to see trends in how you and the rest of the team work. You begin to see how things get done more effectively and with less stress because everyone knows the plan. When you are in this state of mind, or state of work, really, you can begin to get ahead of real time when it comes to seeing trends in your clients, your industry, and your market. Never underestimate the power of planning. It is, in my opinion, one of the biggest reasons that some companies flourish and why, unfortunately, others fail."

Sam handed out blank pieces of paper for everyone to begin drawing their one-line diagrams.

"Brilliant, Sam. Simply brilliant," Jacki said.

"Thanks, Jacki, but it's just a line," he said with a sarcastic smirk.

"Sam, I'm no artist, but this I can do," Jacob said, looking around the room to see how his joke landed. They were all still looking at their papers and must not have heard him.

"One last thing before we start. Each element of the business, each project, and each employee needs one measurement. You see, we need one focal point so we can measure a few different things:

- Where the company is going
- If we are on or off task
- How each person is doing, so we can hold them accountable and manage them toward that one measurement.

"This gives each person the ability to measure themselves. One measurement should always funnel into the big picture. They are completely connected. The question to always ask ourselves is this: 'Is what I am doing getting me closer to the big picture, and is my one measurement moving towards the big picture?' This will always keep you on track. This is the ultimate in accountability. Numbers never lie," Sam instructed.

"Sam, this makes so much sense. It is so typical of us here. We plan things, have strategy meetings, have big ideas, small ideas, and quick meetings, but a lot of times nothing seems to get done, and we can never really put our finger on why. We can't seem to gain any momentum. Now, I understand it. If we were to put these simple, fundamental practices into everything we do and into how we plan, then the execution becomes much more manageable and actually seems attainable. Our meetings will have much more meaning," Jacob said, enlightened by the lines drawn on the board.

"Right on, Jacob. By the way, we are going to talk about how to have effective meetings before the week's done," Sam said.

Andy chimed in, "Sam, this is explosive. I can see how having the salespeople on a plan like this would make life so much easier for them and keep them on track. It is so common for salespeople to get off track. It's funny, they think they are on the right track and it's so obvious they are not.

"With this question, this tool and painting the picture like you said, everything you just talked about will increase their productivity, their one measurable," Andy kept saying it over and over again. "This is going to help me a ton, Sam. And, I think I speak for all of us when I say this is going to help every one of us, especially with each other. Guys, doesn't this seem to answer so many questions about why our meetings seem to end with an empty feeling when we're all just thinking 'what *is* the big picture here and how the fuck are we going to get there?'"

Jacob spoke up, "Andy, you are spot on. This tool gives us the foundation to really keep things in motion."

"And, that is the key, Jacob," Sam began, "*always* keep things in motion. You always want to have motion in action so your people see growth and can connect to the soul of the company. So many companies have their mission statements on their walls and talk about their vision, but if the company doesn't see you moving toward the vision, they don't buy in or believe it is going to happen. Their careers simply become a job, and a means to an end. When you give your people—and yourselves—more of a structure, with guideposts to measure yourselves along the way, for them to measure you, and for the company to measure everything, everyone knows if you are on or off track and where you are headed.

"You know how sometimes when you go on a road trip, the most fun part of it is the car ride itself? You just don't realize it until after it's over and you look back on it," he concluded.

"So true, Sam," Jamie answered.

"I knew you would agree with me, Jamie," Sam said, as everyone rolled their eyes. He continued, "Do you know why this happens? It happens because you all know where you are going, what you will be doing, and when the vacation will be over. You cherish your time together in the car because it's a time you are all together, and it's finite. Those are precious moments where you all share the same inside jokes, laugh about stories, and the hijinks are in full swing. It's the same thing in business. It's like planning a vacation. You need the structure so people can have fun in the process, just like a family vacation."

"That makes so much sense. Sam, you're so good at making the difficult quite simple," Jacki applauded as she sat back in her chair, took a sip of her coffee, and waited for him to continue.

"Simple, yes, but you must be careful not to use this information to micromanage your people. When you have these types of metrics, they are meant to give clarity to your people, but also to empower them to do what they say they are going to do and to bring their best selves to the table.

"Having these metrics also weeds people out of the organization or helps to get them in the right seat, because they know exactly what is expected of them. These metrics and my line that I keep drawing allow you to have tremendous influence over your people. Great leadership comes from this. We will be talking more about leadership throughout the entire week, as we have, but when you have the tools to be a more effective leader and influence your people to stay on course, your company prospers, and your people are happier," Sam said.

Jacob asked, "How do we not micromanage? I find it is very hard to avoid, and there's such a fine line of wanting to know what is going on with everyone and having them think I micromanage."

"Sam, Jacob is right. Sometimes, he can be over the top in wanting to know what we are doing and when it will be done by; to be honest, the entire office feels that way and it's suffocating," Jacki said honestly. Each of the other team leaders nodded in agreement, shifting their gaze from the speaker to Jacob, then to Sam as he began to answer.

"I understand. When you have action items and deadlines, you need to give your people space to work and report back when you have your next meeting or when they need you. *You need to trust them.* This is what builds a trustworthy company. So many times I work with companies where the owners or leadership teams say, 'No one trusts each other around here.'

"The number one reason they feel that way is because they themselves, as leaders of the company, don't trust their people. When you micromanage, it says you don't trust your people. So, Jacob, you must trust your people to do their work, and you must provide the framework we have been talking about. They need to know they can make a mistake and what a mistake looks like. Let them fly, and they will soar. It will seem difficult in the beginning, but just be there for them when they need you. An exercise or best practice is this: make sure your people know their deadlines and let them complete what they have to. When you feel the urge to 'check up' on them, hold off and give them their space. You have the right to inspect what you expect, but make sure it is for them and not for you, or your nerves.

"Now, you can inspect periodically, but don't overdo it. Let them prove to themselves, to you, and to the company that they can do it. When you have the right guideposts and training, the only thing that might surface is that they may be the wrong person for that role. If so, you correct this. This will be a constant in our conversations as we work together through the years." This was the answer that everyone was looking for, and each of them felt much more comfortable going forward.

Now, much time had passed, seemingly in just minutes. What they had now was the ultimate plan they had longed for: to build this company. Jacki agreed to take notes and assemble images of the whiteboard, as well as to create the business plan in one final document. They were so excited they could barely contain themselves.

Sam then continued, "I want to thank everyone for another solid day. I know you worked hard today. You challenged yourselves and let me challenge you as individuals and allowed yourself to be challenged as a group. Thank you for being open to my feedback and each other's, too. Without it, this doesn't work. It is a pleasure working with all of you."

"I can't begin to thank you enough," Jacob said. They had been in the conference room all day and enjoyed their conversation through a working breakfast, a working lunch, and many, many snacks along the way. With only a few breaks and the occasional interruption, the group gelled and felt more like a team than ever before. "What's in store for tomorrow, Sam?"

"That's a surprise! Tomorrow is day three of our five-day transformation. I want you all just to rest up tonight and be ready to attack another exciting day tomorrow. Your only assignment is to arrive sharp, well rested and with an open mind. Deal?"

"Deal!" Jacki yelled out first as she went around the room excitedly high-fiving her colleagues because their firm was finally on the track she had been praying for.

The rest of the team high-fived her back as they packed up their things, thanking Sam as they did. They were on their way to clean up the day and be with their friends and family.

As the team filed out of the room, Jacob hung back.

"Sam?" Jacob interrupted the silence in a low, humble voice.

"Yes, Jacob?"

"Sam, I just … I just … wanted to really thank you," Jacob said with a tear in his eye. "This company means the world to me and somewhere along the way I got lost. I lost my sense of self, and I couldn't find it. If it weren't for this string of wild coincidences —"

"Jacob," Sam cut him off without letting him finish, "there are no coincidences. Everything happens for a reason." He extended his hand to Jacob, "I'm glad I can help."

"You're probably right. Either way, everything that has happened these past weeks and especially these past days has been overwhelmingly incredible, and I just want you to know how much I appreciate you getting me back to me and helping me find my passion and drive again. Words can't express how grateful I am to you."

"Well, I certainly appreciate your kind words. Please know I feel equally as fortunate to work with you and your team. I work with a lot of companies who are successful, but they are stuck just like you. Many of them say they want to grow and change, but they really want to stay right where they are.

"You have a special company with special people, and you are all going to do special things. You are going to attain all of your goals and make all of your dreams come true. Trust me, I know. I see this all the time. I know how to read them," Sam said with a smile as he patted Jacob on the shoulder with pride.

"Jacob," Sam continued, "I want you to remember what I am about to tell you because it's the truth. Your team, the company, the leadership—everyone—they all want to grow. They all want to take the company to infinite heights. But, remember this: they cannot do it without you. They need your uniqueness and your leadership to really lead them. You have a great gift. Use it, and use it wisely. They are depending on you. Do I have your word, Jacob?"

"Yes, Sam, you have my word," Jacob said with an overwhelmed look in his eyes and a deep understanding of what Sam had just said to him. He accepted the responsibility deep into his soul and knew he had a team around him, along with Sam, Dr. Marc, and Aria, to keep him accountable for it.

He stood in the conference room even after everyone in the office had gone home, staring at a picture that his grandfather had given him. He heard his grandfather's favorite song playing in his mind, *Nessun Dorma*, and felt the weight of commitment on his shoulders. He was committed to improving his company and improving the lives of his employees. He took a deep breath, turned off the light, and slowly walked through the door, locking up behind him. Tomorrow was not only day three of their five-day transformation period, but it was the start of a new chapter of the growth of his company.

Chapter 19: The New Culture

*Crave the result so intensely that the work is
irrelevant.*
- *Tim S. Grover*

Jacob woke up the next morning a better version of
himself. After yesterday's event with Sam, he seemed to
have a deeper sense of clarity than he had in years. Maybe
ever. He didn't understand why he had been so aggravated
by minor things for years. The constant internal dialogue he
had with himself had occupied too much of his brain. He
was full of angst. He hadn't been able to get out of his own
mental tornado.

Today felt different. So did the coming days as he
looked ahead. Jacob had a mentor and a guide to keep him
on track—someone he trusted and who would make sure he
stayed on track to achieve his goals. His drive to work was
not typical. He found himself taking a different route,
rolling down the windows to enjoy the crisp autumn air. He
felt he had turned a corner and finally had hope in his heart.

Jacob couldn't stop wondering why Sam seemed to
have such a powerful influence over him and everyone in
his company. What was it? Four weeks before this, Sam
was a stranger to Jacob. If he had bumped into him at the
local drug store or restaurant, he would have walked right

by him. Now, this person played a critical role in his company's success, and even in his personal life. Everything felt surreal.

Jacob was feeling grateful this morning. He couldn't help but think about his father at this moment. Jacob loved his father, but there were so many empty moments where his success in business, sports, and life seemed to go unrecognized by the man who mattered most to him. His father was unable to give Jacob the emotional guidance that Jacob craved.

Sam was the opposite. He elevated Jacob's self-esteem and self-worth that were so important to Jacob's success. Sam seemed to fill the same void for everyone he came into contact with.

When Jacob arrived, he turned off the engine and sat for a moment, composing his thoughts and just breathing quietly for a moment, focusing his mindset for the day.

When Jacob walked in the office, he was pleasantly surprised to see his leadership team already at work, along with several other employees who came in early. Could Sam's impact be even more far-reaching than he thought? Sam had told him that when companies start working with him, the culture immediately begins to shift because everyone sees action and positive movement taking place.

Early on, Sam had said that this is why he needed to meet everyone individually at first, so they felt that they were an important part of the process and that they appreciated that they were part of what was going on behind those closed doors. The team knew that part of this day and the next were dedicated to them, along with rolling out everything they had discussed. When he told all of them this would begin to happen, no one really believed him; but Jacob noticed that people were smiling now. They were moving faster, appearing more friendly, and the vibe around the office just seemed to be happier and more upbeat. As Jacob continued to admire the improved atmosphere, he felt a hand pat his shoulder.

"Good morning, Jacob. Noticing a difference in the company?" Sam asked quietly.

"Yes, Sam. Is it you and the work you have been doing?"

"No, Jacob. It's you and the work that you and your team have been doing. I'll see you at 8:00 in the conference room," he said with a smile as he gave Jacob's back a pat. "Good stuff, kiddo. Good stuff."

* * * *

As Sam walked into the conference room, he couldn't help but recall the first time he felt the way Jacob was feeling that morning. It was many decades ago, and Sam was working with his business coach after a bout of cancer interrupted his life just after he turned thirty. Sam was running a company of his own and was not happy with its direction, or his own for that matter.

He had just been for a routine checkup with his doctor when he heard the words, "Sam, you have cancer."

Like most people, Sam was alone in the doctor's private office when he heard this information. He distinctly remembers the intoxicating smell of antiseptics that day. He remembers feeling numb. Yet, in that foggy moment, he vowed to only do what he was passionate about and what he loved to do. He would no longer live his life in any other way.

With seventeen radiation treatments under his belt, Sam became a warrior of drive, personal awareness, and the impact he had on others, both positive and negative. He began following his own yellow brick road to enlightenment. He knew that letting go of angst and the bullshit of corporate America was in his cards. Sam wanted to grow businesses for a living. He knew his purpose was to help people and businesses grow. Period. The end. He could build a company he was proud to put his name on and whose intent was pure and clear.

Sam was one of the lucky ones: no chemo and "just" a stage one diagnosis of testicular cancer. It's considered a young man's cancer and one of the most curable. He would be able to have children and live a beautiful life, for which he would be grateful every day. He understood how quickly the good fortune of life can be taken from you.

Sam became an advocate for patients. He raised money for cancer-based organizations, specifically Imerman Angels, a one-on-one cancer connection service that brings together people who are going through cancer treatments and those who have already been in their shoes. It was an international organization and Sam's mentor helped him through some very difficult times as he went through his regular CAT scans for five years. The anxiety that comes with cancer checkups and the ever-present worry of the cancer returning was debilitating at times. He could not have done it without his mentor, Jonny Imerman. Sam often thought about where he would be had he not gone through this experience. He often felt it was, strangely, a message from the universe to align himself with his life's purpose. Which is exactly what he did, with the guidance of his own business coach.

Sam knew exactly what Jacob was experiencing right now. He knew the feeling of freedom that came with the unleashing of his new business spirit, plus the clarity about where he was going from here. Sam was excited as his eye caught the leadership team openly laughing and smiling outside the conference room before the meeting started. This company was about to turn a significant corner.

* * * *

The team gathered in the conference room and was ready to go as the clock struck 8:00.

"Team, welcome and good morning," Sam began.

Everyone was sitting around the table with their pens and paper ready. They all responded with an enthusiastic, "Good morning, Sam."

"Okay, let's get started. Today we are going to dive deep into these matters:

- The company's target clients, focus, and messaging
- How you track using metrics, ratios, and numbers, which result in a company's ability to forecast, project, and predict trends in a particular company, industry, and market
- Disruptors and how they will affect your business, industry, and market
- How to have effective meetings
- All the systems and processes within the company, so you operate effectively and efficiently
- And, within all of these, we will talk about growing your leadership and influence skills."

He continued, "Let's start with the company's target clients, your focus, and how you are messaging this to the world. Specifically, to your clients."

This was Jacob's strong suit. After all, it was Jacob who started the company and understood his core focus but didn't necessarily know how to run a company, which is what he was learning from Sam. He had seen and talked to many other business owners about this. They were great at many things, but not at running their own business.

An old buddy Jacob went to Sunday school with, Matt, now owned a very prominent public relations firm. Matt would explain it to Jacob this way, "If you own your own pizza company, you can make the greatest pizza in the world. But, just because you can make the greatest pizza in the world with the best *secret sauce* doesn't mean you know how to run a pizza business." He and his old buddy would often laugh about this. Jacob often felt like the pizza maker.

This being said, Jacob knew *exactly* who his target client was. He knew the company focus and left the messaging up to Jamie, who did an impeccable job of getting the name out there. Sam could tell that the team members were talking amongst themselves. What they thought was perfect, wasn't. Sam could see it, but they couldn't because they were getting caught up in their old patterns of talking.

"Team, let's slow down and stop for a minute," Sam said in a very direct voice. It was his get-your-shit-together voice. "This is how you waste time and get on the wrong track. You need to be able to stop yourself and take a moment to slow down and move with precision.

"Now, I want you to think about how *your clients* see what your core client, focus, and messaging is. Not you, but them. Your clients," Sam demanded.

The room was quiet for a few seconds, and then they all started talking at once. Sam instructed everyone to be silent as he repeated the question. He asked them to spend a few minutes *really* thinking about their answers. He then repeated the question again: "What would *your clients* say about what your core client, focus, and messaging is? Not you, them."

The room was silent for the next five minutes as everyone was deep in thought, jotting down notes. Many of them felt frustrated with the exercise in the first couple of minutes because it was natural for all of them to think, *Sam doesn't even know our business. He doesn't even know what he is talking about right now*. When they hit the third minute of the exercise, they began to realize that Sam was right. They began to see the perspective from which he was coming.

After five minutes, Sam could read the room. He asked Andy to share how he felt about the exercise, and then share his response to the question.

"Well, Sam, I actually think the exercise is more important than the answer right now. Everything you have been talking about was just showcased in the last five minutes. We were all on board to plan and spend executive time thinking about our business. Within seconds we kind of doubted you and jumped into our old ways. Personally, I found that the beginning of the exercise was very frustrating because it was uncomfortable for me. However, once I let it sink in, I started thinking more clearly and seeing different ways of answering the question. What seemed so obvious—and something to rush through—became something to spend time on. Really, it was only about five minutes. How hard is it to slow down and stop and think for five minutes? Team, we need to remember to slow down and take five. Maybe that's where that statement comes from? Who knows? Who really cares? All I know is we need to take five. If Sam wasn't here guiding us, we would have come up with the same old, same old and been on our way down some crazy path where we would potentially have wasted a lot of time because we didn't take five minutes to really dig into the answer."

"Andy, wow! I could not have said that better myself. Like everything, it seems obvious that we need to create some of our own standards. You know, like our own creed that we stand by. If everyone is in agreement, let's start that list," Jacob initiated.

Everyone blurted out, "We are in!" as Jacob walked up to the whiteboard and prepared to write. "What's number one, team?"

Sam watched in amazement as they began to take ownership without his direction. This was an important part of any coaching Sam did. There needed to be a passing of the baton so they knew they could do this without him. It also empowered them to push themselves out of their comfort zone and become better leaders in and for the company.

Jacob wrote "TBM Company Creed" on the whiteboard, with a number one under it.

Next to the first bullet point, he wrote: We will take five minutes to strategize about everything.

The team worked on adding additional concepts to their creed, but the "Take Five" would remain a constant for many years to come. This fundamental concept would help grow the company to infinite heights. They just didn't know it yet. But, Sam did.

"Now, let's get back to the question: 'What would your clients say your core client, focus, and messaging is? Remember: not you. Them,'" Sam asked.

They all continued thinking about and clarifying their answers to this question as well as they could. They thought they knew the answer, but to make sure, Sam gave them one very important task to do these next few weeks: ask *them*.

"Team," he said, "over the next three weeks, every time you talk to a client or a prospect, I want you to ask them the following questions:

- Who would you say our core clients are?
- What do you think our focus is?
- What message are we sending to you?
- Why do you use us?

"The answer to these questions, as well as the others, will expose whether you are on track or off track with your messaging. These answers will reveal how you need to tighten up your messaging, marketing, and branding. Once you have a clear direction on the client's needs and pain points and a deeper understanding of the services they get and want from you, you will be able to provide and service them more effectively. In return, you grow your business in a very big way. Make sense? Can you do it?" Sam asked.

Everyone agreed that it made perfect sense. They agreed that they were all in—they *could and would* do it.

"Team, let's take a break. How long of a break should we take right now?" Sam asked.

Everyone agreed on a fifteen-minute break. What they didn't realize was that this time, Sam didn't tell them they were taking a timed break. He let them decide. This was a subtle yet very powerful way of showcasing that they are in charge, empowered to make decisions. And, they will be able to mirror this ability with the people they manage.

* * * *

The team jumped right back in after what turned out to be a well-needed break to answer emails, team questions, and return a call or two. Sam immediately introduced an important topic that all companies needed to understand and embrace: the importance of metrics, ratios, all company numbers, and how they are used to forecast, project, and predict trends in the company, industry, and market.

Sam began, "Jacob, tell me how you review your metrics, ratios, and company numbers so you can forecast, project, and predict trends in your company, the industry, and the market?"

"Well, Sam, that is an easy question to answer. We don't." This came as no surprise, but it still wasn't what Sam wanted to hear.

"Jacob, if you don't track any of this, how do you measure your growth or your accomplishments as a company? How do you plan for growth if you don't know where you have been and don't have the ability to track past trends and plan for the future?" Even though he knew this would be Jacob's answer, he couldn't keep the frustration from creeping into his voice.

"Well, when you put it that way, it seems obvious, Sam, but as I (and we) have been running, probably too fast, we kind of talked about how to do it and why we should. But, we never had the time—or maybe we never *made* the time—to really understand it and set up any of it," Jacob said. He took a deep breath, leaned to the side of his chair, and continued, "Looking back, Sam, I can see how far ahead we would have been today if we did what you are talking about," he observed before jokingly adding, "Where were you five years ago?"

Jacki took the liberty to speak up, "I worked for a company in high school, and they were so tight, Sam, with everything you talked about. They made everything seem so easy. Actually, they did a lot of what you are talking about now. They were a regional mortgage company that had about forty-five employees. They had the catchiest tagline, "You need it, We—"

"—we lend it," Sam said in unison with Jacki. They both laughed as they sang the jingle.

"Yes! Sam, you know them?" she asked.

"Of course, I know them well ... very well." Sam didn't say that they were a past client, since he doesn't expose his clients, but everyone assumed it because of how intimately he made the comment. The company had downsized after the 2008 recession and was run more like a mom-and-pop shop these days; but, back in the day, they were a force to be reckoned with.

"Jacki, tell us more about that company," Sam suggested.

"Well," Jacki began, "they seemed to have a lot of weekly meetings, huddle meetings, and team meetings, but they all seemed to be very effective and quick. They were really valuable, and everyone seemed to leave the meetings with some type of value, or a talking point, or something to measure as they went back to work until their next check-in meeting. It was an environment that was crazy-busy all the time with so many loans coming in and out of the office every day. But, I would say it was organized chaos, and now that you are talking about measurables and metrics, the entire foundation for this company was exactly what you are talking about.

"That being said, I was a part-time assistant for the CEO and, looking back, they never used any of the metrics, ratios, or other numbers to forecast and plan for the future. I never thought about this before. Looking back, that is probably why got they crushed during the downturn and recession," she explained.

"Well said, Jacki. The recession hit a lot of people really hard. It was devastating for many, but a bit less devastating for those who could feel it coming, who didn't over-leverage themselves, and who understood that the good only stays good for so long and the bad only stays bad for so long.

"Those who had the information and took the time to look at past trends, current and future indicators, and all the news and current events could formulate a forecasting opinion on where their company, market, and industry would be in the next six months to a year. They were in a better place to make corrections in front of the curve, not completely behind it.

"Now, the 2008 recession was an extreme case but, nonetheless, it reminds us that we must be prepared if the market shifts," Sam said.

He then continued with his questions for the meeting, "The questions you all need to ask yourself in order to forecast for the company are these:

- How does your upcoming year compare to the performance of last year and the year before? Why? What are the top three factors affecting this change?
- What will happen to interest rates and Wall Street in the next six to twelve months?
- What economic headwinds will affect your business, company, and industry?
- Will inflation or deflation affect your company and what are the indicators of either happening?
- How accurately have your past forecasts been? Where have you been off? Why?

"It's also important that you understand each metric and ratio of the company so you can answer these questions with the best assumption set possible."

The team spent some time going over every division and every person in the company to determine what metrics and ratios they needed. Jacob took the lead on spearheading this project and asked Andy to work with him on getting it done. The two of them decided to create this for the company.

Once their dialogue was over, Sam noticed something very obvious that they missed completely, "Gents, the two of you are going to take this enormous project on?" he asked, cautiously.

"Yes, Sam, we are on it and excited. Can't wait," came their reply.

"Okay, but, here we are talking about an activity, and you just decided? Right?"

"Yes, Sam," Andy said sarcastically.

"Fellas, you missed something. Do you know what that is?"

"Sam, what are we missing? We did exactly what you told us to do: set up a team to make it happen. That is exactly what we did," Jacob said, a little annoyed at the prospect of having missed something obviously so important.

"Correct. I did, but you missed something, and neither of you can figure it out. Jamie, my favorite student..." Sam said laughingly, "do you know what they missed?"

"Guys, don't kill me, but I do," she said, hesitantly, trying to ease the pain. "You didn't set an action plan with a deadline. You need to look at the big picture, draw the line ..."

Jacob was shocked and quickly interrupted, "How did I miss that? How did we miss that step, Andy?" He felt like a little kid who was just reprimanded.

"Frankly, I have no freaking idea. What the hell is wrong with us?" Andy answered back.

"Seriously, what the hell is wrong with you boys?" Jacki said as she high-fived Jamie with some slick dance moves and a gesture indicating that girls rule.

"Excuse me, all of you, but what the hell is wrong with all of you?" Sam asked in the same joking tone that was in the room. He continued, "Jacki and Jamie, why didn't either of you speak up when you realized no deadline or plan was in place to create a piece that is critical to the mission of the business? This is not a one-person team. This is a team. The obstacle here is for all of you. You cannot just sit back and not voice your thoughts and opinions. You cannot sit back and watch others make a mistake and go down the wrong path. I don't care what the reason. It can't happen. That needs to stop today. Capiche?"

Like a bunch of robots, they all repeated, "Capiche, Sam."

"Let's go around the room right now. I want each of you to commit to having a voice in whatever room you're in, and for the company as a whole. Jacob may be the President/CEO, but without everyone having a voice, you are nothing. Got it?"

The room was silent for a moment.

"I said, got it?"

The team collectively replied, "Got it."

After Andy and Jacob had set deadlines and dates to take on the metrics project, the team took a short break. It was important for Sam to hit a reset button in this room. He deliberately wanted the team a bit frazzled, yet focused, to talk about the disruptors that they may face in their industry or that may even threaten their existence.

* * * *

As the team members made their way back into the conference room after the break, Sam began speaking before anyone was seated. He wanted the team a bit unsettled. He needed them feeling vulnerable. The topic was a serious one and one that most people and companies get sidetracked by.

"Can any of you tell me what happened to Blockbuster, the music industry, and the taxicab industry?" Sam asked them.

"They were destroyed overnight by their competitors," Andy said.

"Their competitors? Is that how you would define them, Andy?" Sam followed up.

"Well, yes, Sam, how you would describe them?" Andy asked, now unsure of his answer.

"Jacki, Jacob, and Jamie: how would you define them?" Sam asked the rest of the team.

Each of the team members answered the same way. They were all on the same page with Andy that these companies were greatly affected by their "competitors."

"Team, competitors are those on your tracking sheets that you monitor every day and week. You monitor them each quarter to determine how you differentiate from them and measure up against them. You are in the market pitching your services over theirs to win business.

"When someone, or a company, comes out of nowhere and destroys you, completely transforms the industry and puts you out of business, that is not a competitor. That is one thing and one thing only: a disruptor. Let me tell you all something, if you don't get in front of your trends like we just discussed, you run the risk of getting run over. Just like what happened to these companies and the hundreds of others that have folded because of Amazon.com, eBay, and so many others that have not even been created yet.

"There are roomfuls of millennials sitting around figuring out how to do something easier, better, more effectively, and in less time. It's happening right now as we speak. Somewhere a group of people is sitting around trying to figure out how to put you out of business. They look at your margins and know they can make a little less, but create a better mousetrap. These disruption-minded people are good people who were raised on technology and have different perspectives on life and business than you do. If you are not in front of this, you will be far, far behind.

"So, the question you need to keep asking yourselves is this: How can our industry and business be disrupted? You should be asking yourselves this question all the time at every team meeting and once a week at company meetings. You will use your indicators and trends to help make assumption sets so that you can set course or change course, as needed. I'm not saying this to alarm you, but so many companies I work with think they will never be affected. More times than not, they are stone-cold wrong. Based on how you answered my initial question, you are behind big time in this thinking. Did I scare the shit out of any of you?" Sam finished talking and grabbed a drink of water..

"Uh, yes, Sam, you did. But you woke me up, and I think you woke up all of us. We need to be thinking about this. It's very real, and we can't take anything for granted," Jacob said.

"I one hundred and ten percent agree, Jacob," Andy said, slamming his pen on the table with a commitment to how he would be thinking about this in the future.

Jacki and Jamie mimicked his action and slammed their pens down, too. They exclaimed, "We're in, Sam. You in?" They giggled, copying the way Sam had been encouraging their feedback all week.

Sam laughed and was happy that the lightheartedness was back in the room after some pretty tough discussions. "I'm in everyone," he affirmed. They all laughed and poked fun at each other's quirks that revealed themselves these past few days together.

"Team, how long is our next break?" Sam asked.

"How about five minutes?" Jacki responded.

The team agreed, and Sam revealed that the next segment would be about putting everything together to begin the process of how to create, delegate, and inspire action and change by way of effective meetings. Something that they—and the company—needed more than they knew.

* * * *

Even with all of the essential information they were receiving, the team did not have a lot of steam left. Sam picked up on this and let them know that the rest of the day would be a bit lighter and more about essential structural elements that needed to be implemented to keep information flowing smoothly. That is where the action happens: with consistent meetings. Let's not have meetings for the sake of having meetings. Let's have *effective* meetings. Sam was going to spend some time now talking about the makings of an effective meeting.

"Let me start off by asking you all about all the meetings you currently have within the company and each division. Let's start with you, Jacob. Do you have a weekly company meeting?" Sam began.

"Yes, I do, but after these days sitting with you, I don't know how effective they are. You have been talking a lot about value, talking points, and insights. It seems as if our meetings are more reporting out," Jacob answered.

"How much time do you spend preparing for your weekly team meeting?" Sam wondered aloud.

"About fifteen minutes before the meeting and also on my drive to work. As the words are coming out of my mouth, I know this is the wrong answer," Jacob said as he uncomfortably laughed and looked around the room at his colleagues.

He continued, "Sam, I need to stop the meeting for a minute and talk to my team. Guys, I need to apologize. I'm sorry for any mistakes I have made these past few weeks. Maybe months. I hate to think it, but maybe even years. They were unintentional. I promise you that you all will have the leadership in me that you need. Thanks for sticking with me. Thank you all so much. You have my commitment that I will not stop working with Sam after this week and I am committed to investing in all of you and everyone on your team. You have my word," he finished as they all kept their gaze fixed on him.

The group and the office knew Jacob wasn't perfect, but they always knew he had a great heart and good intentions. Jacob was one of the most ethical people anyone in the company had ever met. He was one of the nicest people and would give the shirt off his back to anyone. Sometimes, that was misunderstood, especially when he would be firm and demanding, but he simply didn't have the tools. He was learning as he went along. No one could fault him for that, and no one did.

That being said, they were happy to see Sam in the picture, because no matter how positively they felt about Jacob, the company was in a downward spiral and Jacob needed the proper guidance to take his good qualities and run the business properly.

"Jacob, we know you always have our backs. We support you and appreciate you including us in the strategy to grow the company with Sam," Jamie said.

It was a kumbaya moment, and they all felt the unity with one another. Little did they know, this was the beginning of a new chapter that would create one of the most prominent companies in the region and that they all would end up financially secure as equity partners in the company in the years to come.

Sam didn't want to break the moment, so he let it resonate for a bit until it was time to move back to the topic of having effective meetings. But, first gave his two cents about what was happening in the room.

"Support and take care of each other always. You do that, and everyone wins," Sam said having a newfound pride for everyone in the room and for what was being created.

It reminded him of summer camp, where very special bonds are created. If you have experienced it, you might not be able to describe it in words, but it's magical. Sam experienced it at Tamarack Camps in Ortonville, Michigan. Jacob was a Tanuga kid, which was a camp in Kalkaska, Michigan. Both were rugged camps, and each of them had made lasting friendships there. In these past fifteen minutes, a camp bond was created among them that would last forever.

"What just happened was amazing. I know you all felt it," Jacob said after a while. "Let's get back to talking about meetings. Sam wanted us to talk about the meetings we have. We'll rate how effective they are on a scale from one through ten."

Each person went around the room and spent a good five minutes going over each type of meeting they had with their team and with each other. The overall rating was about a six, but everyone voiced their intent to get to a ten.

"Okay, well you may not be able to do a ten each meeting, but we will do our best to get you close to that. I am confident you will all embrace the challenge to get better at hosting meetings, especially once you learn the fundamental formula of a good-quality, value-added meeting. It appears as if many of you are having meetings for the sake of having meetings now, so it's time to change that."

Sam continued to tell the team, "Let me tell you all something. There is nothing people hate more than a meeting for the sake of a meeting. They have no value, and people feel micromanaged and that all you want to talk about is useless bullshit. It's a distraction, and people have no interest in disrupting their day to go to your meeting. I am going to make meetings very easy for you."

"Love it, Sam. I love easy. I think we all do," Jacob said.

Sam continued, "Let me ask all of you a question. What do you think makes an effective value-add meeting?" Sam pointed to Jacob, the leader of the company.

Jacob was a bit uncomfortable in answering the question because he thought he had the answer, but now he wasn't so sure. He was so used to the status quo of his meetings. No one had ever told him differently. So, he answered, "I agree with what you said. They need to be meetings that provide value."

"I hear you, Jacob, but how do you define value? More importantly, how do *they, the attendees* define value?" Sam followed up.

"Hmm," Jacob laughed, "Sam, it seems so obvious, but I can't seem to come up with the words. Maybe, more value? Guys, help me out here ..."

Everyone was a bit stumped. They had gone so long with just having meetings where people reported their activities and progress. That does serve a purpose, but doesn't always keep the ball rolling. They were stumped, and they knew it.

Sam finally cut in. "Okay, let's break down the fundamentals and the formula. What makes a meeting that people consider worth coming to? Here is the formula:

- Talk about the issue of the week. These may be internal issues or market issues, or both
- Provide insight into solutions
- Provide ways to think about the process and solutions
- Provide talking points to your team for clients on the issue(s)
- Provide a forecasting solution that everyone can get ahead of for themselves, the company or the clients.

"In summary, every meeting should address hot topics and provide talking points to help your team transition their thoughts into conversations with their team or with clients. You are the leader of this, which means you have to take everything that is going on in the office, in the market, in the industry, and in the world and find a way to wrap it all together and give your people a way to make it conversational.

"The goal is to be a conversation in their everyday communications with their teams, colleagues, and clients. Every meeting should have this. Every meeting. Along with all of this, you need to be clear about what your message is for every meeting. It is also helpful to have a theme for every meeting so that people understand what the meeting is about and can compartmentalize the material in their minds after they leave."

All eyes were glued on Sam. Everyone nodded in agreement. "What happens more often than not is that even though people are smart, they have so much going on in their lives and business that they don't fully understand how the information can be streamlined into a conversation that fits within their business. You can help this by doing a few things:

1. "Be a resource to provide talking points on a plethora of topics.

2. "Always be the resource to provide them with 'what's next.' This can be in their everyday projects or how to take their client relationship to its next level. You become this resource when you have effective meetings because your team sees you as the leader, the visionary that knows how to make them better. It's that simple.

"When you take this level of ownership and leadership for your meetings, you begin to set the tone for a new level of quality. By the way, it takes time to prepare and have these types of meetings. The reason you don't see many people having meetings with this type of quality and depth is because they are just winging it. If you are a leader in a company, you never want to just wing it. You always need to prepare, at the very least, an outline of what you are going to talk about. This should not take away the spontaneity of your meetings, but you need to start with an agenda, and you need guidelines for what you will be talking about.

"When you do this, you are more focused, which in return gets your team more focused. You see, the reason I like short meetings is because there is only so much an individual can retain in one sitting. There is only so much information or guidance they can absorb. So, if you are focused and clear on what you want from someone, and can provide value on how they can give it to you through short, focused suggestions, you all win," Sam finished. He took a long drink of his water and a quick bite of a muffin while waiting for them to reply.

"Well, Sam, I can tell you that my meetings have none of that as of today. But, starting now they will," Jacob responded. He was a great student and could implement swiftly once he had a solution that made sense. It was something everyone admired about him. He also could inspire others to do the same and follow his lead.

"Team, we on board with this?" he asked.

They all nodded their heads and agreed.

"How do we prepare and stay in front of everything you just talked about?" Jacob asked Sam.

"I want all of you to create an Excel document. You'll either use a new tab for every week or have an ongoing stream in one cell that you date each week. Keep this on your desktop and every time you find that little nugget of information or hear of something in the market, your business, or the company, write it in for that week, so you have an ongoing stream of that week's happenings.

"You might be wondering what these little nuggets are. Well, we're looking for any kind of valuable information that is current. It's what's out there right now: complaints, or issues, or problems … anything that you can present to your people. You want to address these things at your weekly meeting and give people a different perspective on them. They are talking points that they can take into the field with them, and they will turn them into something productive.

"When you create the spreadsheet, you can divide the cells by company, market, industry—whatever makes sense to you. It doesn't matter. Do what you need to do to document the information. Once you have the information, you can choose how you want to organize it for your upcoming meetings. Each meeting will require you to present a bit differently depending on your audience and the direction you are taking in the meeting.

"The key is to have all the issues and information at your fingertips so you can prepare accordingly. Nothing will slip through the cracks and you ensure that everything gets addressed that needs to get addressed. Every meeting you have with your people should touch on at least one piece of business, even if it is small.

"I'm not saying that you should skip any social conversations, but there should be some type of business element to every real conversation. Even if you ask them how the X-Y-Z deal is coming along. They don't want to be micromanaged, but they want to know you are always engaged in their business.

"When you are walking and talking with your people, you will be able to get all the information you need to understand what is going on with them—and the company—as well as where they need guidance. The consistent messages are what become your themes for the week. If you want better themes or want to know more of what is going on, you need to become better at asking questions. This will be something that constantly evolves in our ongoing work together. I will guide you on the power of asking more effective questions so that you can get more information—better information—that will help you grow not only the company but your people as well."

"This makes a lot of sense, Sam. Sometimes I feel as if I'm talking to my people about too much personal stuff. There's a disconnect that comes with that. I always thought it was odd, but because we are creative types, I thought it was important to be this personal. I thought I had to connect with people on a more personal level. I felt that was important. As I look back on recent conversations with my people over these last couple of weeks, had I peppered in a comment, question, or thought during those conversations, they would have appreciated it. I'm sure of that," Jamie said.

"Exactly, Jamie. They want it. There is a fine line between always talking business and micromanaging. If they trust you and you let them do their work, they don't feel micromanaged, but always want to know you're connected to what they are doing," Sam told Jamie. "Does anyone have any questions?" he asked.

"Sam, what types of meetings should we be having as a company?" Jacki asked.

"Important question, Jacki. All companies have different types of meetings they should have; you as a team need to decide what is effective and ineffective for your company and divisions. But overall, here are the critical ones:

- Monday morning sales meeting to kick off the week with the company
- One to two training workshops per week
- One to two team meetings per week. These depend on the teams that need to meet
- Salespeople should have weekly meetings to track their activity and growth
- Five to ten minute effective huddles as needed
- Mandatory weekly leadership meeting."

He continued, "These meetings should always be on the same day and time each week so that everyone can plan accordingly." Sam emphasized the word *plan*. Planning is important to everyone in the company and is an essential element of holding meetings.

He went on, "I also like meetings that are ten to forty minutes, maximum. If you have a strong agenda, message, and action items and a deadline, then get everyone back to work, that's ideal. The best meetings are those when the leaders facilitate conversation and participation. Those will be your most exciting meetings and those that your team likes best. If you are prepared and know what you want to talk about, you will be able to facilitate the conversation with ease. That being said, it's not easy to get tired people talking on a Monday morning, so you have to bring your A+ game on those days," Sam laughed.

"Remember this: always give them a new way of thinking about things, provide the next steps, and give them some talking points to take into the field. You'll have the makings of a successful meeting."

The weekly leadership meeting was an important meeting for the team to begin having right away. They needed to connect on the issues affecting their business, the industry, their people, and market indicators. These meetings would be used to prioritize the issues they needed to attack, set action items to get them done, and give them a space to talk about solutions to hot topics or issues they needed to be aware of. These weekly meetings would prove to be critical in keeping the action in motion.

Sam then continued to speak, "There are some other meetings you should think about having, too. Jacob already told me you don't have these. Among them, there should be these:

- A yearly kickoff. This is a meeting that wraps up the previous year and sets the vision, message, and theme for the upcoming year.
- Quarterly one-on-one meetings with each person in your department. You should also have quarterly one-on-one meetings with each other.
- Quarterly leadership meetings to recap the previous quarter and plan for the upcoming quarter. These should be off site with a facilitator so you get below the surface and can really grow your business in a big way.
- Yearly business plan meetings to map out the upcoming year and recap the previous year.

"I would also recommend that you attend one or two seminars a year, or at least take them online. This should also be available to all employees of the company. Continuing education is tremendously valuable and should be promoted in any company. Outside resources are huge for your employees' personal development which, in return, grows the company and everyone in it."

"Sam, all I can say is that these are some quality ideas that will make a huge impact on our business, not to mention, give us a much more organized way to grow the company," Andy commended Sam. Jacki, Jacob, and Jamie all agreed. Excitement was written across each of their faces.

"Andy, you said the key word, which is 'organized.' It is an organized way to grow the company. We have talked about the importance of planning. With planning comes the need to be organized in the way you approach everything. Everyone wants and needs structure. Without it, it's too hard to know what to do next. We talked about assembly lines and the power of how they work so well. This is the same thing. The more of an assembly-line structure you put into the company, while keeping the spontaneity alive, the faster you will grow and the more fun you will have.

"You don't need to know how to implement all of these today, but as we continue to work together, I want to see all of this in your company. Jacob, I think you should have a kickoff in January, and you should begin planning that now."

"I would love to do that, but how?" Jacob said.

"I like to keep things easy, so if you're following this process and back it up with a killer PowerPoint, plus solid content, you will create the vision for the whole year for everyone in the office. This is a presentation where all the department heads speak, as well. You want the entire company to connect with your vision."

Sam proceeded to draw an outline on the board for them to use when planning their kickoff. This is what he wrote:

- Theme for the upcoming year
- Go around the room and compliment everyone on one positive thing they brought to the company. Follow this by saying, "We have the right team—the best team—to accomplish our goals."
- Past year in review and lessons learned (as needed)
- The new year's business plan, the vision for that year and a company overview review
- Three to five year plan and projections (as needed)—Quick, high-level summary with few details (if needed)
- Ten-year plan and projections (as needed)—Quick, high-level summary with few details (if needed)
- Headwinds discussion (if needed)
- A complete competitive analysis and how you differentiate yourselves
- Recap in summary and infuse excitement that you are going to kick ass in this new year."

He then began to explain the outline.

"This is another formula to use when you are having meetings. It doesn't have to only be a kickoff at the beginning of the year. This is actually the perfect foundation of any good meeting, with some modification depending on the meeting and its purpose. You will be successful if you use this structure and, of course, always be yourself when you present.

"Speaking of structures and being organized, it's time to talk about systems and processes before we end the day. Let's take a –"

"Fifteen minutes!" Jacki yelled out.

"Okay, then!" Sam said. Despite the intensity of the week so far, everyone was in good spirits and ready to complete the remainder of the activities for the day.

* * * *

As they continued their meeting, Jamie asked, "Sam, do you have a business coach?"

Chuckling at the question, Sam replied, "Everyone asks me that question. Of course, I do. I've had a few in my life, but the one who was the most impactful was Jules Stewart. He is really one of a kind. He has helped me more than any single person I have ever worked with. His perspective on everything was always so spot on. He saw through all the bullshit, could ask the most pointed questions, and get me to my next level, over and over again. He always had my best interest in mind, and he always had my back.

"He has become a close friend over the years, but when we are talking business, he is my business coach ONLY. He never mixes the two. He pushed me hard to grow, and he is one of the reasons I still have such a zest for my own personal growth and for my business. I'm the type of person who will never retire. I may slow down a bit, but I'll never retire. Jules is the same. I have been using him for thirty-plus years, and I'm very grateful for his guidance."

"Jules sounds great. He must be very proud of you as a student," Jamie answered back.

"He is, Jamie. He is." It was in that moment that the group could see a bit of Sam's vulnerability and his imperfections. Even *he* had a coach to work with on his own growth. They felt more connected to Sam than ever, adding to the love and appreciation they already felt for the man of such wisdom, such an ability to change lives.

"I learned from the best!" Sam exclaimed, gazing beyond them as he recalled his mentor. He went on,

"Enough about me, let's get back to all of you. It's been a very productive day. We are going to end the day with an assignment. It's not a homework assignment, but an assignment that will revolutionize your business. It will tighten up your progress faster than anything else you can do because it will save you all time. When you save time, you can focus on what is important and at the core of what you *need* to be doing. Remember, we talked about your unique superpowers? When you find the time and space to do more of that, you begin to grow your company without even realizing it.

"All we have is time. Our time has to be protected every day. It is precious. If you think about all the time that people waste, it's no surprise they can't get anything done in a day or say they feel like they are drowning. Once you do what I am going to suggest to you, you will be able to really understand all the gaps in the company and where you need to hire more people, realign responsibilities, and how you can utilize and leverage technology to give you and your team more time."

"Sam, I'm chomping at the bit. Please tell us," Jacob pleaded.

"What we're talking about here is having all the proper systems in place and creating all the proper processes within the company. The systems are the technology that everything runs from and the processes are the step-by-step methodologies directing how everything gets done. It's the ultimate form of accountability and communication because it's the backstop determining how everything is accomplished. It's the ultimate standard of who does what, why, when, and, most importantly, how it all gets done. When we have this as a company, we begin to use technology the right way, so it works for our team, our company, and for our clients. This allows the company to service everyone more effectively, so we can be the ultimate in efficiency and run like a well-oiled machine.

"One of the biggest complaints I get when I work with companies is that they have no training when you come on board. This is because most companies don't have any systems and processes that streamline what they do, so training is always on the go. You learn by shadowing someone. The obstacle is that, as a company, everyone has their own spin, their own understanding and their own way to teach something. That's all fine, but when there is no foundation of how to teach, everyone ends up learning it a bit differently, and there is no consensus on what is being taught.

"Also, companies have turnover. Sometimes a lot of turnover. When you have nothing in place, you have to start from scratch every time you hire someone. Often, you have someone who is not well trained themselves to train someone new. And now you are creating mediocre people. This becomes a vicious cycle.

"To create this—and implement it—takes some time. That is why I suggested it is an assignment. It is one that we need to put to a timeline and set deadlines for; but, the first task is to understand exactly *what* needs to be systemized and what needs to be put into a process. Once we have the outline, we go to work and create it all. The obstacle here is that most people say things like, 'We don't have the time to do what we need to do,' or 'We can't add this on top of everything else we do.'

"Here is the solution: *you must find the time*. I can't be more direct or firm than that. *You must find the time*. There will never be a good time. *Ever!*" Sam shouted.

He then continued, "This is one of the most fundamental, most powerful things you can do with your company. By the way, there are many people who don't mind training, but no one *loves* training, especially if they are not getting paid more to do it or some kind of bonus at the end of the year."

Sam looked at Jacob, suggesting that the two of them would continue this conversation later. "Team, listen: there is a reason McDonald's is so successful. When you buy anything at McDonald's, everyone understands *exactly* what to do at every step of the process. You must follow that example."

The team was visibly overwhelmed. No one knew how they would find the time.

Noticing their hesitation, Sam finally asked, "Team, you tell me: how are we going to do this and get it done?"

"We really need to rally together here, everyone," Jacob began. "We each need to commit to small steps. Sam told us that if we do small things every day, we get big results. We subscribe to the same mindset. First, let's talk about how long the overall process will take. I'm thinking it's a six-month project from initiating the thought process to creating to rolling everything out. Jacki, what do you think?" Jacob asked as they turned their attention to their bubbly office manager.

"I think six months sounds about right. This will allow us to do it right. I was initially thinking three months, but six months gives us time to really brainstorm, work it out, do proper research, and tackle any mistakes, instead of rolling it out too early, making mistakes, panicking, and having to rewind everything," Jacki answered.

"I agree. That sounds good to me, too. That being said, there are many things that won't take six months, and we need to figure out the ones that can be done quickly as we map everything. You know, so the employees see the action in motion," Jamie chimed in.

"Are we working as a team, or what?! I agree with everyone, and I'm on board with making everything work to get us to our goal," Andy said.

"Okay, team!" Jacob confirmed excitedly. He felt like he was taking a step toward a new level of leadership in the organization, a role for which his desire had faded some time ago. His employees had been waiting for that desire to return. Right now, his leadership team was seeing that unfold right before their eyes. Everyone could feel Jacob's excitement. Something had shifted for him. Sam could tell he was in the process of feeling like his old self again and regaining his lost connection with his company.

Sam sat back and enjoyed the conversation as they, as a team, worked out a complete timeline of who would do what and when, plus what teams would be created and how they would roll out the initiative to the company.

They divided up each department and assigned tasks to determine all the necessary systems and an outline of all the processes that needed to get started. They created deadlines and initial goals and even found small chunks of time to ensure that tasks were going to be completed. They were well on their way. Sam knew this would be an ongoing conversation between him and the team as the months went on; but, for now, they had it under control, and Sam wanted to empower them to create their map on their own. He sat quietly while they worked, interrupting only once to offer direction.

"Well, well. You are working like quite a team! How does that feel?" Sam eventually asked the group.

Jamie jumped in, saying, "*Amazing,* Sam! Absolutely *amazing*! I think *we* all have been wanting and craving this type of collaboration but couldn't get here on our own. It just seemed to magically happen."

"I love magic!" Sam said with a boyish smile. Sam got so excited when he witnessed how his teaching transitioned from them thinking they couldn't do anything without him to them forgetting that he guided them and gave them many of the tools they needed to get there. This was an important step in the week-long transformation. Part of the process was to get them to feel like everything was *their* idea, not his.

Sam faded in the background as the team spent the next fifteen minutes recapping their plan, as well as what they had learned and accomplished that day. Without asking, the team pushed each other to create action items with specific deadlines for all of their outstanding issues. It amounted to pure joy for Sam and the others as well. They had become a stronger unit and, because of that, were better equipped to lead the company.

The team now understood the power of systems and processes in a business. The execution would take more effort, but they were up for the challenge. They knew they had each other, and Sam, to keep the action in motion.

Someone noticed that it was now after 5:00 p.m. They had been in the conference room working hard *the entire day*.

"Day three is done, team. Well done! You were all incredible today! Kudos to all of you for your hard work. We got a lot accomplished. Now, the key is to focus on execution and no excuses. You can correct the course you have set, but no excuses. You should all be very proud of yourselves," Sam exclaimed to the entire team.

He continued, "Tomorrow, we will be discussing many of the things that businesses forget to talk about and putting everything together for our company-wide meeting on Friday. Everyone in the office is going to be very happy to hear what we have been talking about this week, and they will definitely be happy about the changes they will be seeing in the weeks and months to come.

"Like I said, no excuses. Once you put it out there, your employees need to see action in motion or *everything* will backfire on you. We don't want that to happen. Now, on a scale from one to ten, how would you rate today's meeting?"

"Ten," Jacob said.

Andy piped up, "Ten, Sam!"

"An absolute ten," from Jacki.

"An eleven!" Jamie said with a huge smile.

"I would expect nothing less from my favorite student," Sam said with a wink.

They packed up and left the office by 6:00 to enjoy the evening with their families. Tomorrow's topics were going to be just as effective, and Sam wanted everyone well-rested and completely focused. He told them to get a good night's sleep. They would resume again at 8:00 a.m. sharp the next day.

Chapter 20: Branding and Marketing

What gets measured gets improved.
- Peter Drucker

The team gathered in the conference room, ready to start their fourth day together. They could not believe how quickly the week had gone. Could it be that, just a week ago, they had none of the tools that they now had which they so desperately needed to transform their company?

Jacki was the first to speak, "Guys, listen, I have been thinking a lot about what Sam has been teaching us, and I started getting a little nervous last night. We have *a lot* of work to do, both individually, and as a team. I'm nervous about all of us doing the work, finding the time to do the work, and making sure we do it right. Not perfect, just right. I'm nervous that we may fall into old patterns as soon as Sam leaves. Do any of you feel this way, too?"

"I hear you, Jacki. Setting business plans for me, the company, my salespeople, the systems, the processes, the this and the that … it all got me wondering, how are we going to attack all of this?" Andy asked the group.

"I was feeling the same way," said Jaime. "It was frustrating because, in that room with Sam, everything felt so possible. So do-able. So much easier than it does once we are left alone to get back to work."

Finally, Jacob spoke up, "Listen, team, I have the same concerns. But, we are going to make this happen. We are going to take it in small chunks and make sure we are doing a little every day. That is our pact with one another. Just a little every day. Let's not try to bite off too much. If we do, then we will set ourselves up for failure.

"Part of holding each other accountable is in understanding where we are, where we want to go, and helping each other get there one small step at a time. We cannot have unrealistic expectations of each other; yet, we need to push each other to do what we say we are going to do. That is why we need our weekly leadership meetings.

"Sam will be emailing us an agenda to follow so we can keep things in order and keep the ball rolling. When we meet with Sam today, we will tie up all these loose ends into some type of plan for us to follow. Everything is going to be manageable. You'll see. We can do this, guys! I know we can!" The confidence in Jacob's voice made the others relax.

The team continued to see Jacob as the leader they had known when they joined him almost five years ago. This was the guy they admired. This was the guy they wanted to work for and hoped to one day partner with. This was the guy who would lead the change with confidence, conviction, and moxie. He would infuse the company culture with positivity and a growth-based mindset. They had their guy back. They had their leader back.

"Hey, everyone, *you in?*" Jacob demanded, sounding exactly like Sam.

The team shouted out, "WE. ARE. IN!"

"Alright, then," Jacob said, pumped, "let's make it happen!"

"Hey, Jacob, you sound exactly like your old self *and* like Sam at the same time," Andy observed.

"Well, Andy, I feel like my old self again. As Sam would say, I learned from the best."

* * * *

When the clock struck 8:00, the team and Sam were in the conference room to start day four. Sam greeted everyone as they walked in, "Welcome back, everyone. How is your morning?" Everyone looked down quickly. They didn't want to let Sam in on their secret meeting before meeting with him.

Sam continued to talk, "If you are like most companies I work with, you have probably been flipping out since we parted ways yesterday. You were probably all freaking out because you think there is no way you could accomplish *any* of what we talked about, even though it seemed so easy yesterday when you left, and you were all leading the charge of change. Am I on or am I off in my assumption?"

Jacki answered, "Sam, are you a witch or psychic or something? That is exactly how we all feel. We just had an impromptu meeting before this and we were trying to figure out how the hell we are going to do all of this. Jacob, our fearless leader, calmed us down and set the stage for how we wanted to start the meeting today."

"How would you like to start the meeting, Jacki?" Sam asked her.

"We want to just recap everything that we've talked about and set realistic timelines, deadlines, and what individuals are going to own each piece in order to accomplish it all. We also want to figure out who is leading each piece of the project," she answered.

"Music to my ears, Jacki. I'll bet that the last twelve hours have been really, really stressful. Am I right? Was it a new feeling?" Sam responded.

"Yes, Sam, a totally new feeling. And you're right on all fronts," Jacki confided.

Andy and Jamie chimed in agreement that it was a very stressful time since they walked out of the conference room the night before. It was indeed a totally new feeling for them.

"Well, let me tell you all something. That stress was *always* present. You just didn't realize it. It was happening under your feet. That is how your employees feel when they don't know what is going on or they see random acts of change with no consistency. That is the fear they feel. Also, that disconnect of structure, planning, and organizing created an undetectable stress in your company walls and in its culture. You just didn't realize it because you didn't know what to look for or who to listen to.

"Now that you are seeing things with open eyes and hearing things with fresh ears, you are simply exposed to what has been there all along. That is what day four is all about: creating your new normal. That is exactly what is going on. If I do my part the right way, and you do yours— and we both have—that is exactly what I expect you to feel after day three is done and day four begins. It is, as we like to say, the *measurable* of how our work together is progressing. We struck all the right nerves, and now we are on the path towards growth and change. Big growth. Big change."

"So, this is normal, Sam?" Jacki asked.

"One hundred percent normal. And expected. Great job, everyone, for getting to this place. It's not easy. It can be a rough time, but it is where excellence comes from. In my entire career, I have only had two clients cancel after day three because they couldn't handle the realization of just what kind of effort it takes to change. They paid me in full for the week and told me they couldn't do what it would take—they didn't *want* to do what it would take. They did not have the strength or the energy to fix and refix their company. They assumed they would move along in the status quo and remain complacent. How do you think they ended up?"

"Not very well, I would imagine, Sam," Jamie answered.

"Not well at all, Jamie. They both went out of business within twenty-four months," came Sam's reply. Then, he continued, "They gave up. In business, you can never give up. Giving up is not an option. You must always be looking forward. You must always be growing and keeping up with the changes of where your business will be. You need to be the change makers, not the ones who get destroyed or left behind. It is a commitment and a daily challenge. It's not easy; if it was, everyone would be doing it."

"Did you all see the movie, *A League of Their Own*?" Everyone replied that they had, and how much they loved it. "Do you remember what Tom Hanks' character says to Gina Davis' character when she wants to quit because it's hard?" No one could remember the line.

Sam continued, "He said this: 'It's the hard that makes it great.' And what you experienced all last night is the hard. I had an old friend and mentor, Steve, who used to say that line all the time. He was a good man. When he fell on hard times, that line got him through to the other side. Now, the question is this, how much effort does it really take to make the 'hard' possible? The answer? Just a little every day. Because when you do a little every day, it compounds over time. Everything compounds: the good and the bad.

"It's like that question, 'Would you take one million dollars today or a penny that doubles every day for thirty days?' Many people are quick to take the million dollars, but a penny that doubles every day for thirty days is worth 10.7 million dollars on day thirty-one. It's simple math, but very difficult to comprehend. Everything compounds, even the small stuff.

"Too many people are all or nothing. Do everything in one day, or do everything in one week. What happens is that they never find that day or that week and all of a sudden months and years go by and nothing's done. If they were to simply do a little every day, it gets done and feels like, as you would say, Jamie, 'magic!'" Sam said as he motioned that he had nothing up his sleeve.

"I want you all to take out two clean sheets of paper," he requested.

The team did what they were told. "I want you to draw four columns on the paper. At the top of the one on the far left, I want you to write 'Issue.' On the second one, write 'Solution/Action Item.' On the third one, write 'Result(s).' And, on the one at the right, 'Who Owns it/Deadline.' Now, write the issues you are having in that first column, the action item that you need to take, then the results you want to see. Lastly, in the final column, indicate who will own this and what the deadline is. By the way, before you start, please note, you now have the power to create your own solution map anywhere, from a coffee shop napkin to a blank piece of paper to a computer spreadsheet. I'll be quiet now. Please begin."

Sam sat back in his chair as he watched everyone write madly. Sam watched the anxiety in the room dissipate as the minutes went on and they continued to write out their solutions map. After ten minutes had passed and everyone was looking up, Sam asked, "How was that exercise?"

"Huge for me, Sam," Jacki answered. "I must say, I was the one who probably was the most stressed out this morning. Or, at least the one most vocal about it. This put me at ease and gave me a way to lay my thoughts on paper and create an action plan at the same time."

"Great to hear, Jacki. So often we listen to ourselves and the voices in our heads, when really we need to stop listening to ourselves and start *talking to* ourselves. This exercise allows us to talk to ourselves and quiet those voices in our heads. It lets us get our business voice back and brings our business mindset back into the picture. Do you see the difference between talking to yourself versus listening to yourself?

"The thing is, the voice you are listening to is typically stuck in old patterns and in old ways of doing things. It will drive you crazy because it is only using the resources it had until you learned something new. It messes with your mind and puts a lot of self-doubt into your psyche. Like I said, all of this takes effort. You and the team have to be ready to put forth that effort and be ready to truly shift your mindset. I have said it before, and I will say it again, if you can't shift your mindset, you won't see the optimal results," Sam concluded.

"Sam, that was profound and spot on, I wish I would have heard that twenty years ago. It would have saved me a lot of the senseless bullshit that I put myself through," Jacob said, looking Sam directly in the eye. "Thank you for sharing that. I think it is so common that we listen to the bullshit stories we tell ourselves; and, many times, I know in my case, they are stories I don't want in my head in the first place. They were ingrained in me from my mom or dad or grandparents or friends or TV or random people. Any, and maybe all, of these sources sent me a message that I owned but never intended to. I think what you are telling me is that when that voice is in my head, and I'm listening to it, I need to tell it to shut up and start talking to myself. I need to tell myself the new story and stop getting stuck in the past," Jacob said.

"Jacob, that is exactly what I hope everyone takes from this," Sam responded. "Team, is that what you took away from that story?"

The all nodded in agreement. They loved the way Sam always threw his thoughts out to them, but this in particular resonated with them on the deepest of levels. Sam knew and understood when to share just the right thing at the right time so it would have the right impact and create important change, not only in their business but also in their psyche.

The next part of the morning was dedicated to setting timelines, deadlines, action items, and gaining an understanding of every project and task they had talked about over the past three days. The team broke everything into bite-sized chunks and assigned each one a realistic timeline. The follow-up meeting was set, and everyone knew what they needed to do to get it all in motion. The room was energized by their acceptance, understanding, and appreciation for having worked through it all together. They felt united and were looking forward to their follow-up leadership meeting next week.

Andy asked for a short break at this point, and the team took the opportunity to clear their heads for the next part of their meeting. Sam, however, was preparing to stretch their mindsets even further.

* * * *

Sam began their next session by saying, "Okay, team, now we are going to talk about some important extensions to your business plan. I like to talk about them as add-ons because most people don't think about them as part of their business. But, they are very much a part of everything you do on a daily basis. I like to focus on this *after* the business planning sessions have taken place because it is easier to understand how to layer these into your plan. This is better than doing it all at once when it is all so very new. Right now, we are going to discuss this:

- Your recruiting business plan
- Your marketing and branding business plan
- Your technology business plan
- Your strategic partnership business plan

"These are critical to the growth of your business, but I always find it interesting that most business owners and companies attack these on an if/when basis and they don't have an actual plan in place to use these tools to grow their business all along.

"I think you understand what recruiting is, as well as marketing and branding. With technology constantly changing, you need to always be reviewing your current and future technology needs, in order to stay ahead of the curve and your competition. Strategic partnership may be a new phrase for you, though. A strategic partnership is something of reciprocity. You refer clients to a company or a certain professional who can help grow that business in a certain way, and then if that company or professional has a client who could use the goods or services you provide, then you would be the referral. It's about helping each other grow their own businesses and help their respective clients, too.

"Most people are quite reactive instead of proactive when it comes to these four plans. If you want to grow your business, always be looking at ways to be proactive.

Especially in areas where others are reactive. This will
allow your proactive plan to crush your competition."

The team loved when Sam made comments like *crush
your competition*. It got them very excited, and in the
moment, they all understood that there was enough
business for everyone to be successful, but why not aim to
be the best? Why shouldn't they crush their competition?

Sam looked at Jacob, "Tell me how you and the
company have approached these four types of plans in the
past?"

"Well, Sam, I hate to sound like a broken record—and
a slightly embarrassed one at that—but we haven't. We
haven't approached them at all. We are the people you just
talked about who take a reactive approach to everything.
We don't recruit unless we have to. We don't think about
marketing and branding unless we have to—as a company
that is. We do plenty of marketing and branding through
Jamie and her group, but maybe not as strategically as we
think we do. We don't spend enough time assessing and
upgrading our technology. Our strategic partnerships
happen by chance—they are never planned.

"We have never sat in a room and thought about who
would be a good fit to align ourselves with. It just seems to
happen through networking events or random

introductions. Again, no plan to speak of. Jamie, what do you think?"

Jamie answered Jacob's question, "Jacob, I would agree. I mean, I spend a lot of time on marketing and branding our inventory and our company name, but as we sit and think about it, I don't know if we have ever had a marketing and branding *meeting* per se where we plan everything out and really compose some creative messaging. That seems odd considering I run the marketing department and we seem slammed every day, pushing out content all the time on a daily basis. As I'm sitting here talking, I can't even believe we haven't had this discussion before. Of course, we *should* be planning, and we *should* have a strategic marketing and branding campaign. We need to get people's attention and maintain it—for our current clients and our new clients.

"The good news is, I'm on board, and it sounds like a ton of fun and way more productive for our creativity. Forward thinking and proactive instead of settling for the same old, same old. Which, by the way, much of our competition does. This will give us a leg up in no time."

"Jamie, that is dead on. What about your social media marketing and branding?" Sam followed up.

"Same. No planning, no strategy. Just postings. Now that I think about it, we are doing nothing different than our competition. It's no wonder people sometimes can't understand why we are different from them—it's our fault. We have not done an effective job to market ourselves. We need to prepare. We need to have a plan of attack, and we need to execute that plan of attack on a consistent basis. Would this be a topic for our weekly leadership meetings?" Jamie asked.

"Exactly, Jamie. You may have been on the wrong track, but now you are on the right one again. Can you see how these weekly leadership meetings will keep the constant flow of communication and accountability intact?" Sam said.

"Absolutely, Sam. It seems so obvious, yet so brilliant," Jamie responded, a bit starry-eyed.

"It's both. In summary, it's simple but takes a commitment. When you meet regularly and set a plan of attack *each week* that will be reported on the following week, a lot gets done, and the leadership team is all on the same page. This is how things begin to move forward, and you and your company begin to see change and growth. And you will see that trust grows within the organization. It's a beautiful thing to experience," Sam said calmly.

"Let's talk about training and recruiting for a few, shall we?" Sam transitioned the conversation smoothly.

He continued, "It's quite simple: you must *always* be recruiting. It's really that simple. At your quarterly meetings and even at other times when you review your company as a whole, you must always know who you need a Plan B for. You should always know which of your people may be unhappy and choose to leave.

"There are those who you wish would leave, and those who you might need to kindly ask to leave. Then, there are those who may leave when you want them to stay. In any case, you need to be in front of this situation, and you need a strategy for dealing with it. This is why it is critical to review your team at each leadership meeting.

"If you are always recruiting, even when you don't think you need to, you never leave yourself in the unsatisfying position of keeping someone in the wrong seat for too long. You have a solution already behind them. I watch so many companies keep the wrong people for years or even decades because they don't make the time to recruit on an ongoing basis. They don't have a Plan B.

"Whether it's having a constant recruiter, ads on websites, or just asking people to refer good, solid individuals, it should be a large part of your business plan.

Also, it's good for the team to see that you are interviewing. It reminds them of their mortality, so to speak, so they hit the standards that are expected from them. As the company grows, it is important to have people to hire at your fingertips when you need that extra admin person or someone to jump in when the work piles up. This strategy helps everyone on the team grow.

"The best way to create a plan for this is for each of you to review your people. Look carefully at where you will be in six to twelve months, and recruit accordingly. Remember this: you must always be recruiting, training, and retaining good people.

"We talked earlier about creating a training manual so that when you hire the right recruits, it will be used to help them train themselves in addition to the mentor or mentors you provide for them. Everybody on board?" he asked with the words they had become so accustomed to.

Everyone said with a smile, "We are on board, Sam."

"Great. Let's move on and talk about marketing and branding. I have an old friend, Nick, who always says 'Life is marketing.' I have always agreed with him. It really is about how you package your product and market it over most everything else. Is anyone in this room old enough to remember Billy Blanks and Tae-Bo?" The question was odd, but they were able to recall Mr. Blanks' shadowboxing workout routine. They all chuckled and nodded.

Jacob was the first to speak up, "I remember Billy Blanks," throwing a hook and a jab as he said it. "He reminded me of Mr. T. 'I pity the fool...'" Jacob said in his grittiest voice. They all laughed, more at him than with.

Sam refocused the group, "He understood marketing. Tae-Bo was kickboxing renamed with brilliant marketing. Do any of you know the definitions of marketing and branding?"

Jacki answered, "Why people buy your products?"

Andy said, "Name recognition?"

"Promoting your name and what you sell?" said Jacob.

"All of the above?" came Jamie's response. They all seemed confident yet insecure in their responses.

Sam sat back in his chair and let them finish talking. He leaned forward and put his elbows on the table in front of him, saying, "Let me tell you what my definition is for marketing and branding. Branding is what people say about you when you leave the room; marketing is the consistent message you send to people about your brand."

He continued, "You have the ability to control your brand through your marketing. On a side note, we all have an internal brand and an external brand. You need to manage both. This is important to monitor as you grow the company. It will be particularly interesting to see how your brand is after our meeting, when you start implementing changes and compare it to what it was before we started this metamorphosis.

"We will continue this discussion at many follow-up meetings. In summary, marketing and branding should get more clients through the door and keep your current clients coming back. It can be hard to measure, but you need to find ways to measure it. Often, the relationship brings in the business, but it's the marketing and branding that support that relationship. Many think it's just the relationship, but in many cases, it is everything you do as a whole company to bring the clients through the door. That is where the business comes from. The clients.

"Now that you know what marketing and branding are, it's important to take time and create a marketing and branding plan, along with an editorial calendar for social media. I think it is best to do this on a quarterly basis, at a minimum. We also need to take a look at email signatures, letterhead, and everything that has your name and messaging on it. Jamie, do you want to take the lead on this and set up a team and a meeting to create this particular business plan?"

"Yes. I'm already taking tons of notes. I have lots of thoughts about this. Andy, I would like you on the committee with me because of your influence with the salespeople. You in?" Jamie asked.

"Of course I'm in," Andy responded.

"Great. I'll email you some dates after the meeting to get started and set our first meeting early next week," she told him.

"Perfect. Thanks for taking the lead, Jamie, I appreciate it," Andy said.

Sam spoke up, "Now this is what I like to see: teamwork and collaboration amongst departments without Jacob or me telling you what to do. Well done!"

The team then spent time reviewing and committing to expand their technology at their weekly meetings; fully committing to doing their best to stay on the cutting edge for the ultimate client and employee experience. Sam then moved the meeting along saying, "Now, let's move on to your strategic partnership business plan.

"This is the fourth part of almost everyone's business. Usually, no one thinks about it. We need to create a plan for strategic relationships. It is very common to generate business from strategic partnerships, but they always seem to happen organically. What I am asking you all to do is take out the worksheet in the booklet I gave you at the beginning of the week. It says, *Strategic Partnerships* on it. On that sheet, you will see about twenty lines. I want you to write down all the business relationships you have. That would include the ones you want, and the steps you are going to take to build your next five. Put deadlines on each one and write down what the result will be from creating that solid, strategic relationship as well as the power it has to grow your company and theirs."

"Sam, I feel like a broken record, but focusing on these is absolutely brilliant. I know so many business people, and I don't think any of them do this. If they do, they don't talk about it. Maybe they think it's obvious, or maybe it's their secret weapon. I have always heard that what you focus on, you get. And, this planning takes it to the next level," Jacob said to Sam.

"I'm glad you find it useful, Jacob. Note that executing it and keeping it consistent in your business planning will be the challenge, it always is."

Just as they were finishing up this discussion and recapping the four new business plans that were brought to their attention today, a late lunch was wheeled into the conference room. Sam had lunch brought in each day so they could keep working and maintain their momentum. He wanted to keep the group together and make sure they broke bread together, too. Every nuance was important to building a team, and Sam watched as they communicated with each other. As the week progressed, lunch hour chats improved. They became more casual, more honest. They were trusting each other more.

Sam left them to talk amongst themselves today. He no longer needed to observe the lunch conversation. He preferred to sit back and let them create their own conversations and build their relationships on their own. Everything was working as planned. Sam now prepared for the next segment: how to roll all of this out to the company.

Sam addressed the team, "Now comes the tough part. Rolling all of this out and giving the office an inside look at what we have been talking about these last few days. The reason I meet with everyone individually, as I did with you all, is because you want them to be part of the process. Nothing builds distrust more than some outsider coming in, like me. The employees have no idea what my intentions are or why you brought me here. Then we sit behind closed doors for days. All they can assume is that they are going to get fired and lose their job! It's scary.

"In this case, they saw me come in. I connected with each of them, and you fired two people. But, those people were toxic. The employees wanted them to leave. Remember, it is your responsibility to take care of people. Sometimes, you have to take some difficult steps to maintain a safe environment that can flourish and grow.

"Keep in mind that everyone fears change, too. We need to roll everything out to them and be completely transparent, but they don't need all the details and frankly, they don't want all the details. Overall, they want to see all of you taking and spearheading consistent action. They need the big picture, not the minutiae. We need to be tight, direct, transparent, and informative without getting into the weeds. People mostly want to hear what is going to be done, who is going to do it, what role they play, and how their job description is or isn't going to change. What they also want to know is whether they are getting a raise, a bigger bonus, or maybe a nice chunk of profit sharing at the end of the year.

"You need to be prepared to answer these questions with solid answers to avoid building distrust. And, boy, we do *not* want that. Tomorrow is a very big day—one that your office has been looking forward to. I know this because I see it everywhere I go. And, I have been talking to these people all week during our breaks and at the end of the day.

"So, let's plan it out: what exactly are we going to roll out tomorrow? Who is talking about what? Who is the leader? Please talk amongst yourselves; let's figure out the immediate agenda, roles, and responsibilities of each of you in the room."

The team set to work, diligently creating a very detailed and transparent agenda. They decided Jacob would take the lead. Andy would lead the presentation to the salespeople, Jamie would lead the marketing and branding talks, and Jacki would address how the office was going to be involved. Jacki would take the lead in getting everyone on committees, helping everyone set agendas, and keep everyone and everything in motion. The team was so excited to announce their new initiatives to the company. They talked about how the soul of the company has been rediscovered, and they all felt more connected to this operation than they had in months.

Jacob looked at Sam while they completed the assignment with a little help from their mentor. This is exactly how Sam wanted it. They all had the power, instincts, and knowledge to do what Sam had taught them. Most of what they heard wasn't new, but clearly the students were ready, and the teacher arrived. They were proud of themselves, and Sam was proud of them, too.

He was especially proud of Jacob for allowing himself to be vulnerable in front of his employees and for having the courage to open himself and the company up to growth and change. He knew how difficult this was. He recalled being in Jacob's shoes at one time, and how he, too, had struggled. Those struggles had brought him to this place in his own successful career. It was a moment of complete satisfaction for Sam, as it was for this team of leaders who delighted in having regained control and were now steering a fresh course toward success.

Sam then addressed them, "Team, I am so proud of you! More importantly, you should be proud of yourselves. Let me review a few things now you need to keep in mind as you present to the company tomorrow.

"Remember to be authentic. They want you to lead them, but they want you to do it as the people you are. Remember that this may be the most important meeting of your career because you are launching the company's next chapter. It is your responsibility to lead the charge, all of you, as a team and as individuals. Remember that the way you lead, walk, talk, move, get excited, handle stress, and manage disruptors will set the tone for ninety percent of

your company, especially you, Jacob, as the owner and
CEO.

"All of you hold these responsibilities on behalf of
your people. You want them to come to work every day,
and you want them to not only bring their best selves but to
do the best job they possibly can. For you, and for
themselves. They all want to be a part of something bigger
than themselves, and they have chosen to do that here.
Don't make them regret it—now, or in hindsight. Give
them what you want: a place to flourish, ignite, and grow.

"Tomorrow, I want you to speak from the heart. I want
the employees to connect to you and the company on a new
level like they have never before. And they will never
experience it again anywhere else. Be the leader that
inspires the best versions of themselves. You all have the
power to do this. You are all special in your own way. They
are lucky to have you! And, I have been lucky to have had
you, too.

"Thank you for your time, wisdom, participation, and
courage. Each and every one of you. What you did this
week wasn't easy. I promise you. I am better for knowing
all of you, just as each of you is better for knowing the
others. And your employees are better for having been led
by you. Thank you, thank you, thank you.

"Tonight, I want you all to practice. Know your agenda and your talking points. Be ready for tomorrow. The meeting that lays the foundation for your vision and company growth starts at 8:00 a.m. sharp, and breakfast for the entire office will be available starting at 7:30."

Jacob was the first to respond, "Sam, first, let me say on behalf of all of us, THANK YOU! I personally don't know where to begin. You saved me," Jacob said as a tear began creeping down his cheek. "You saved me, and you saved the company, Sam. I know you won't take any credit, but I was lost—we were lost. I know it was mostly my fault. Maybe all my fault. I am grateful that our paths crossed and—let me make this clear—Sam, we are never letting you go! You are truly part of this team, and our work together is far from done." He stood and extended his hand toward Sam's.

"I am honored. I'm looking forward to working through all of the future challenges with all of you. Now, pack up and go get some sleep. You need to be fresh and sharp for tomorrow," Sam said, as he, too, felt his eyes moisten. This relationship he had with Jacob and Jacob's leadership team was deeper than most others. Maybe it was the team or the company. Or, maybe Sam was just more selective when it came to choosing clients as he got older. Whatever the case, it was a perfect match.

Jamie, Andy, and Jacki all stood up and gave Sam a huge hug and thanked him for everything he had taught them this week.

Andy said, "Sam, I love ya, and I know I was your *real* favorite, not Jamie." They all laughed as they left the conference room once more, excited for tomorrow's company meeting and the big reveal.

Chapter 21: Company Meeting

The only place success comes before work is in the dictionary.
- *Vince Lombardi*

As the meeting began the next morning, Sam sat at the back of the room and watched his students become the teachers who would lead the company to its next level and beyond. He watched their excitement and joy as they presented their vision, ideas, and action plans, as well as their explanations of how they came to many of their conclusions at their weeklong meetings with Sam. They were transparent in describing their errors and missteps, and they were honest and forthright in explaining their roles. Watching the leadership team in action was a beautiful thing. After all, it was just a week earlier that they had so very little direction. Now, they carried themselves with confidence and conviction. And they were working as a team.

Sam also admired the faces of the employees, whose eyes were filled with their own sense of excitement and anticipation. They sat and listened, mesmerized, as they discovered exciting changes taking place and that they had an important role to play in all of it.

The presentation was outstanding. Everyone was genuinely connected to their team, and it seemed that they all had a much deeper connection to one another, and to the company. As the team finished their different portions of the presentation, they asked Sam to say a few words.

Sam walked up to the front of the room humbly, as though receiving a lifetime achievement award. He was quiet and subdued. He didn't want to take much of the credit for the leadership's transformation.

He addressed the crowd softly, "I love what I do for a living. I get to watch transformations take place in front of my eyes. I get to spend my days being a student and a teacher. I teach, but I also learn from everyone I work with.

"Let me share with all of you what I learned from your leadership team and from all of you. I learned that being open to change is a gift you cannot buy. You are all open to change, and you are open to growth. You don't see that in many organizations. I'm talking *real* change. This is the kind of change that is hard. It takes time and forces all participants, from the top down and the bottom up, to get gritty. To get their hands dirty. This is the kind of change that requires extra courage and the ability to be vulnerable. This change puts you in an arena that many are scared to fight in. This is the change that makes us better people.

"The reward for this kind of change is a renewed company, focused growth and for each of us, our own personal advancement. All of you taught me that this still exists. Moving forward, it won't always be easy, but nothing worth having is ever easy. I promise that you will all have open communication along the way because your leadership has committed to it. This will make obstacles more manageable. There will always be a way, even when it seems there is none. We are all here for each other. I am not going anywhere, and I will continue to be here for all of you, too. You need to make me one promise, though," Sam said with a smile, "you need to do all of this, but you also need to have fun. Promise me you will have fun!"

Every single one of them knew Sam's shtick, and together they said, "We promise we will have fun." He always liked ending his talks on a light note and was pleased with their laughter.

He carried on, "I applaud you all. Thank you for letting me into your world. I am grateful. I will never let you down, and I am always available to each of you when you need me."

With those words, Sam turned the floor back to Jacob, resuming his post at the back of the room as the leadership team finished up. Sam was used to, and enjoyed, being the guy behind the people. He preferred it. He never needed the credit and was fulfilled by letting other people shine in the light he helped to create. It was his purpose. He did what he loved, and that was enough to feed his heart and his ego.

Sam continued to watch the company completely transform before him in mindset and connection. The body language, attentiveness, and active participation in the room was magnetic. Everyone was pumped up for the change, and they were, as he liked to put it, completely on board.

When the meeting was over, Sam stuck around and talked to many of the employees. He got a kick out of how excited they were for all of the changes and growth about to happen. Sam mostly listened—they didn't have many questions for him—and assured that he would be there for them, whether they had questions, needed direction, or to brainstorm strategies. Sam assured them, as did Jacob, that Sam would be a staple in the company for years to come and made sure everyone had direct access to him. This provided an additional layer of trust because they knew they would have a balanced voice—from the company and from Sam.

As the conference room cleared out, Jacob and Sam found themselves alone, just like the first day when Sam came to the office.

Sam spoke first, "You did it, kiddo! You have come a long way, and Dr. Marc would be proud of you. You fought those demons, and you won, my friend. You got your head on straight again and got your mindset back. You can't buy that at any store for any price. *You* did it, Jacob. You. Did. It. I hope you are as proud of yourself as I am of you, Champ!"

"I'm speechless! I don't know where to begin, and I'm so overwhelmed with gratitude," Jacob stammered. "THANK YOU! THANK YOU!" Jacob said as he firmly shook Sam's hand in an enthusiastic grasp before throwing both arms around him in a big bear hug. "Thank you, Sam, you have been the mentor, father figure, and voice of reason I have needed. I can't wait to tell Dr. Marc all about this week. He will love it."

"Oh, I know Dr. Marc and he *will* love it even more than you think. I need to take him golfing and thank him for introducing me to you. He hits a mean drive, that Dr. Marc. One great dentist and one helluva golfer!" Sam said.

As Sam was walking out the door after their week-long metamorphosis, he looked at Jacob and thanked him once more. Smiling, he said, "Again, Jacob, great job today. You and the team knocked it out of the park. I'll see you for our team follow-up meeting?"

"You got it, Sam. Looking forward to it," Jacob replied.

"Me too, Jacob."

As Sam walked out of the office, Jacki, Andy, and Jamie were all waiting to say their goodbyes. He didn't mind seeing them one more time before he left. As he was walked to his car, his cell phone rang.

"Hello, Sam?"

"Yes, this is Sam."

"Sam, hi. My name is Robert. Dr. Marc gave me your name and number. We need your help," pleaded the voice at the other end.

"Hi, Robert. Great to talk with you. Tell me what's going on and how I can help you?"

Chapter 22: What Really Matters

Realize deeply that the present moment is all you ever have.

- Eckhart Tolle

Jacob awoke early the following Saturday, invigorated by the week he had at work. What had started two months ago as a monumental undertaking was now coming to completion. He knew it would take massive amounts of work to get there, but he was no longer afraid of the outcome. He knew that if he took Sam's advice to just do a little bit every day, the results would come. He trusted in it.

As he turned on the coffee pot, there was another order of business he needed to attend to. He grabbed his phone and deftly composed a text to Joanna, "Hey, just confirming we're on for dinner tonight?"

He placed the phone on the countertop, whipped up a bowl of cereal, and waited. Within minutes his phone buzzed with her reply, "Looking forward to it." She even added a smiley face. It was a date.

After spending some much-needed time at the gym, Jacob took a quick shower, turned on the Michigan football game, and decided to call Dr. Marc to fill him in on the week's events. He dialed Dr. Marc's number, listening to the dial tone.

"Hello?" Dr. Marc answered.

"Hey, Dr. Marc, it's Jacob. How are you?" he asked.

"I'm well, Jacob. How are you?"

"Great!" Jacob said excitedly.

"Sounds like it. I hear things went well with Sam," Dr. Marc said.

"To say things went great would be a gross understatement. That guy is a straight shooter. He will tell you exactly how it is. And, he doesn't let you get away with anything. Within five minutes of meeting each other, and me not having my shit together, he called me out on it. Definitely something that I needed!" Jacob said.

"That's exactly why I connected the two of you. Sometimes, Jacob, we need people like that in our lives, and even more so in our business. How did the week go?" Dr. Marc asked, encouraged by Jacob's honesty.

"Well, Doc, I know I haven't always been the most willing to seek or accept help. It finally feels like I am getting to the other side of the hump. It's going to be a lot of work, but, now, working with Sam, this train is finally starting to see the light at the end of the tunnel."

Dr. Marc cut in, "Don't get ahead of yourself, Jacob. You have only met with Sam for a week. There is still plenty of work to do, I am sure. Don't forget that."

"Oh, yes. Yessir. I know that. There's a long way to go. How about this? At least I feel like I'm back on the tracks, no longer derailed. Is that better?" Jacob said, amused at his own wordplay.

"You really are in a good mood, aren't you?" Dr. Marc said, sticking it to Jacob a little bit. "I can't remember you having been this light and jovial before!"

"I feel good. This last week has been very enlightening. I'm excited for the path my company is now on. Plus, to add to the excitement, I've met someone." Jacob revealed this little detail, even though he had only known Dr. Marc for a couple of months. Dr. Marc had a way of making anyone feel comfortable. Like a great uncle who sits around telling stories, making all the little cousins feel like he's their best friend. There was a sense of comfort in the dentist that Jacob liked and, because of this, he did not mind sharing his little secret.

"Jacob, that is great to hear. There's one thing that I know, beyond a shadow of a doubt, to be true: Life is much more enjoyable when you share it with another person instead of going it alone. If you think this young lady is special, then my advice—whether you want it or not—is to hang on to her. Don't let her go, and enjoy every minute you have with her," Jacob could hear Dr. Marc's voice begin to shake, just a bit, as he surely was thinking about his late wife.

"Thanks, Dr. Marc. Hey, why don't you and I go and get dinner sometime? No work talk. No mentoring. Just us hanging out. How's that sound?"

"I would like that very much, Jacob. How about next week? Say, Thursday night?"

"Sounds great. I'll drive. I'll even pay this time," Jacob said, sarcastically. And with that, they hung up.

* * * *

Jacob made one little detour on his way to pick up Joanna for their night out. He stopped by the local flower shop and bought her a dozen roses. He had never done anything like this for just anyone; in fact, he could not remember the last time that he had personally bought flowers for someone. Usually, Jacki handled that. Today, however, he was buying them for a woman who he cared for, a woman he loved. He wasn't even completely sure he knew what that felt like, or what it looked like. But, he knew there was something different about her, and he was going to hang on to her as long as he could, according to the advice of Dr. Marc.

Their relationship was relatively new. It had only been about a month of casual dating and no talk of what was going to happen next. That was mainly Jacob's fault. He was very noncommittal, especially when it came to relationships. He had never allowed himself to get tied down to anyone, more married to his work than anything else. Tonight that would all change.

As he pulled up to Joanna's apartment building, he felt the butterflies take flight inside of his stomach. With a sweaty palm, he unclipped his seatbelt and opened the car door. The night was cool and dry, and the light breeze whipped at his cheeks as he walked to the front door of the building.

Inside, he buzzed Joanna's apartment, and she opened the door for him almost immediately. He made his way up three flights of stairs, eventually landing at her doorstep.

As she pulled the door open, Jacob caught his breath. She was dressed in a black dress that fit her perfectly. Her golden hair was tightly curled and pulled to the right side of her neck. The sun glowed from behind her, casting her outline in a silhouette. Jacob had seen this happen in the movies, but never in real life. As this angelic image stood before him, he was completely speechless.

He blinked a few times, swallowed hard, and finally mustered up the courage to mutter two words, "Uh, hi." She giggled in a way that could have knocked him over. This was the one. This woman standing in the doorway was the one that Jacob knew he'd be spending the rest of his life with. He had never thought about this before, but right now, he liked the thought of it.

"Wow," is what came from his mouth next. Then, he remembered the flowers hiding behind his back. He handed them to her.

"Jacob! They are beautiful! Thank you," she said with a smile, clearly excited to see him and for the evening ahead. "Come in for a second, so I can put these in water before we go out." They both stepped into her elegant apartment and Jacob took a seat on the couch. He had been wondering how to bring up the idea of a steady relationship with her, and now seemed like the perfect moment.

"Hey, Joanna," he began, "before we go out, I wanna ask you something."

"Okay?" She said, growing curious.

"Have you given much thought to an 'us?'" It was bold, but this was unchartered territory for Jacob, so he went with it.

"I have, a bit. It's hard not to when we've been going out for the last month or so. Why, have you?" she asked flirtatiously.

"I have," was his simple reply. "I've never given much thought to relationships." This was coming out wrong, and he knew it. "Um, what, er, what I mean is this: I've always been more concerned about my work. I've never really thought about serious relationships. But, over the last month, I've realized I have never met anyone who would give me a reason for wanting to settle down. Until that night we first met at the Oak Tree Tavern."

That was all he needed to say, apparently. As he finished that sentence, Joanna slid next to him and kissed him, preventing him from saying another word. Tonight was the first night Jacob and Joanna would head out the door as a couple. Their first night of many to come.

* * * *

The night that began with such promise only continued to get better. Jacob had secured them a coveted window table at The Whitney. The Whitney is a Detroit gem, a converted mansion offering the most elegant dining experience. Jacob was pulling out all the stops tonight. This was officially their first date. And, the transformation of his company was going so well that he had plenty of reason to celebrate. And celebrate they would.

Dinner was perfect. Afterward, they made their way up the stairs in the old mansion and had a drink at the Ghost Bar, a perfect end to a perfect night. As the familiar sounds of Van Morrison's *Someone Like You* were filling the space around them, Jacob leaned in and kissed Joanna. She leaned back, smiling, and said, "Well, thank you for that." He smiled and just nodded.

"Joanna, tonight has been perfect. Thank you," he said.

"No," she said, "thank you. This is all so wonderful." She placed her hand on his forearm, sending goose bumps all the way to his shoulder. As the music played, Jacob stood up and held out his hand. There was no dedicated dance floor in the Ghost Bar, but that wouldn't be stopping him. Not tonight.

As the two of them danced, Jacob broke the silence, "So, next Saturday night, my buddy Fish is having some people over for a party. Would you like to go? They are all great people, and they would love to meet you."

"I would love to meet your friends," she said.

"Great. Pick you up at 7:00?"

"Yeah, sounds great." They finished their dance, and Jacob drove Joanna back to her apartment. He left, giving her one last kiss for the evening. Everything this week was going Jacob's way.

* * * *

Everything that had happened this week was exactly the kind of break that he had been seeking for months.

There was plenty of work that needed to be done, and meetings to schedule, but he needed to make sure he did not bite off more than he could chew at once. On Thursday, he and Dr. Marc went to dinner, and had a great time, but as the week ended, Jacob was ready for what the weekend would bring; this weekend was when Joanna would meet his friends.

On Saturday afternoon, Jacob sat back in his leather chair and rested his head. As he closed his eyes, he remembered the night this all started. He remembered the darkness closing in around him as he sat, alone, in his office, with just his lucky Titleist to keep him company. He remembered Aria, and what a great friend she had been, not just through these hard times, but ever since they met in college. She would be at the party tonight, and he was excited that she and Joanna would finally meet.

It was time for him to pick up Joanna. He hopped into his car, put on his favorite Pandora station, and made his way across town to Joanna's apartment. She answered the door in jeans, boots, and a brown sweater, perfect for a cool fall day in Michigan.

"Hi!" She greeted him with a kiss, turned to lock the apartment door, and walked ahead of him to the car. He couldn't help but notice that no matter what she wore, whether dressed for the office or a night out, she was a knockout. He smiled at the thought.

They talked and laughed non-stop. Jacob loved hearing Joanna laugh as they exchanged stories about their workweek. They held hands the entire way, neither wanting to let go of the other.

They arrived at Fish's party, excited to see everyone. Jacob made all the introductions, and they claimed a spot on Fish's couch. Most everyone was more interested in the girl who had finally captured Jacob's attention than in the game or each other. Everyone, including Aria, was impressed with Joanna, which came as no surprise to Jacob. Aria and Joanna bonded through their mutual love for *Gilmore Girls,* reviewing all of the favorite episodes and characters.

By the time the party was over, Joanna was clearly welcomed into the group, which was just icing on the cake of a great week. Everything was perfect. Jacob felt happy and, finally, completely fulfilled.

Chapter 23: The First Three Months

Some people want it to happen. Some wish it would happen. Others make it happen.
- Michael Jordan

As the months passed, Jacob's team had been working hard to implement everything they had discussed with Sam. This allowed Jacob to sleep soundly at night. As Jacob stirred from his sleep, he was up earlier than usual. He could not wait to tackle the tasks that lay before him and his team. Quickly completing his morning routine, he grabbed his coffee before heading into work.

Even though it was early, he dialed his brother Geoff's number. They had always had a tight relationship, more like good friends than squabbling brothers. Sure, they sometimes argued—all brothers do—but they always had each other's back.

"Hello?" Geoff answered gruffly. He was surely not out of bed yet. No surprise.

"Hey, buddy," Jacob said, clearly more awake than his brother.

"Is everything okay? Why are you calling me this early?" Geoff asked.

"Everything is fine. I just hadn't talked to you in a while, and I wanted to see how everything was going." Although they talked fairly regularly, both of them were very busy with careers. These conversations happened less often than they should have.

"Everything is good here, Jacob. Kids are good, wife is happy."

"Well, that's part of why I'm calling. I wanted to share a few things with you. First, I haven't really told you this at all, but I was burnt out in my business. I was actually ready to give the whole thing up."

Geoff cut in, "What? Why? Is everything okay?"

"Yes, yes. Everything is fine. Now. But it wasn't. A couple of months ago I was ready to be done. I had no direction, no fire, no reason at all to continue. I didn't call you about it, because I figured I would fight my way through. Aria helped me out and turned me to someone who hooked me up with a killer business coach."

"You? You hired a business coach?" Geoff didn't mean this to hurt his brother when he said this—and it didn't—but, it was a bit of a shock considering that Geoff *never* knew Jacob to ask for help from *anyone*.

"Yes. I know, big shocker. But I'll tell you what: it's the best thing that I have ever done. Sam's guidance put my company and me right back on the track towards success. Obviously, nothing's happened overnight, but it's going to happen." Jacob was a bit surprised by his own confidence. "And, there's something else: I've met someone. Her name is Joanna. I wanted to wait to tell you about her, because I wanted to see if it panned out, and it definitely has. You guys are going to love her."

"Well, that is something, brother. You really do have some good news to be sharing. Say, why don't you come by sometime. It has been way too long, and I know the kids are missing their uncle."

"I would love to, and I'll bring Joanna," Jacob promised.

Geoff sounded genuinely excited when he said, "That sounds great! I'll text you some dates later today, and we'll get something in the books. I have got to get the kids going, we're running a little late. Some things never change."

"They never do," Jacob said, "Alright, Geoff, we'll set something up. Love you, man."

"Love you, too." And with that, they hung up.

* * * *

Jacob made his way into the office and noticed that he was alone. He took out the pad of paper on which he had done his planning the night before. He began to organize his notes for his meetings later that day. The office started to fill with cheerful voices around 7:45, and this made Jacob smile.

The first few months had gone smoothly. The leadership team had knocked it out of the park in their team meetings, and the buzz around the office was excited and contagious. The team had taken everything Sam had suggested, as far as meetings went, and ran them efficiently and effectively. Each of them could barely contain their excitement as they reported back to Jacob, and each was excited for another of Sam's follow-up visits on Wednesday. They worked tirelessly to be prepared for the meeting.

The rest of the week played out similarly. The leadership team was handling the transformation flawlessly and, by Thursday afternoon, Jacob was ready for his monthly dinner with Dr. Marc.

As he prepared to leave for the day, Jacob's phone rang. The caller was identified as "Rick Bloomberg." Jacob set the phone down and grinned.

Uncle Richard.

Rick Bloomberg had followed Jacob's career when he first got into brokering commercial real estate deals, and had handed him his first listing. Rick was a quiet, sharp, wise, older man. Jacob would never forget the first piece of advice he gave him when he entered the business: Show up every day.

Rick would tell him, "If you show up every day, everything will work out." These past few months had not been easy, but had he not recalled the sage advice and thrown in the towel instead, he would be in quite a different place now. At that moment, Jacob thought back to three other pieces of critical advice he had gotten from his Uncle Richard and his business partner Denny:

- Always be well capitalized
- Always stay liquid
- And, don't overleverage

This advice had saved all of them a lot of heartaches and helped Jacob through the ups and downs of business. Rick was famous for driving all over the state of Michigan, cigar clenched between his teeth, as he scouted properties to buy and sell. Even at the ripe age of seventy-five, he was still making his rounds, working his beat in the real estate game.

Jacob answered the phone and was greeted by Rick's articulate voice. Over the years, their paths no longer crossed as often as they once did, but Jacob continued to be grateful to have Rick in his life. He had been a major force in Jacob's start in the business. It was always reassuring to hear the familiar voice, especially as his business was continuing its transformation.

After hanging up with Rick, Jacob left the building and got into his car. Tonight was going to be a type of "thank you" dinner for Dr. Marc for introducing him to Sam.

He met Dr. Marc at the dentist's office before heading to the restaurant. Their evening included a great dinner and even better conversation. No talk of work, for either of them. Jacob got lost in Dr. Marc's stories, like a young Jedi at the feet of Master Yoda. While Dr. Marc spoke, Jacob sat back in his chair and thought about this man sitting across from him. He smiled at how randomly they had come together. Or, really, was it random at all?

Part Four:
The Evolution

Chapter 24: The Proposal

If you don't know where you want to be in five years, you're already there!
- Unknown

The seasons shifted from fall to winter, winter to spring. Spring. The season of rebirth.

Jacob's business was shifting, as well. Things were moving along quite well. Change is never easy, and this one was especially challenging. They were heading in the right direction. Today, he was meeting with Aria, but the focus of their conversation would not be about business. He had something else to talk about today: Joanna.

He and Joanna had now been together for about six months, and it had been the best six months of his life, he thought. She loved him, and he loved her. She made the difficult times of his business transformation much easier to deal with and had supported him every day. She allowed him to vent if he needed to, and she celebrated the small victories, too. She was the exact person that he wanted by his side today, tomorrow, and the rest of his life. This was what he needed to talk to Aria about.

As he made his way to the bakery where he and Aria were meeting today, he wore a smile the entire way. Nothing would bring him down today.

He arrived at the bakery fifteen minutes early, so he called Dr. Marc while he ordered a coffee.

"Hello, Jacob," Dr. Marc answered.

"Hey, Doc, how's your day going?" Jacob asked.

"Not too bad, Jacob, not too bad at all. The practice is going well, and I'm thinking about taking a little trip. You know, just to get away for a bit. How are things going with the business?"

"Things are going great! The team has taken everything Sam preached to us to heart, and we have made great strides over the last couple of months," Jacob said, very proud of the progress he and his team had made. It had not been perfect, nor had it been easy, but with the tools given to them by Sam, it happened much more smoothly and easily.

"That's great to hear, Jacob. Say, why don't you come over to the office in the next week or so? I have to run now, but we could grab a bite to eat and catch up some more," Dr. Marc offered.

"That sounds great. I'll be there. Just wanted to let you know, I'm going to be asking Joanna to marry me. I'm telling Aria today. In fact, I'm meeting her in a few minutes. I just wanted you to know, too."

"That's great, Jacob! I want to hear all about it when I see you. Talk soon, Son," Dr. Marc said and hung up the phone needing to get to a patient who was in a chair waiting for him.

As Jacob put the phone down, Aria joined him. She sat across the table from him and smiled.

"What's going on?" Jacob asked suspiciously. He had not told anyone about his plans, except for Dr. Marc, so there was no way that Aria knew what he was up to.

"Oh, nothing," she began, "let's order. Then you can tell me exactly how you're going to propose to Joanna!"

Jacob looked like he had seen a ghost. "Relax, Jacob. It's no surprise. We've been friends for how long now? I know you like the back of my hand, and I could tell you were going to pop the question the moment I met her. She is perfect for you."

"I'm that predictable?" Jacob wondered.

"Jakey, you're more predictable than the sun rising in the east every morning." That stung, but Jacob laughed.

They went to the counter and ordered, then returned to their seats where they spent the next hour discussing various topics and that in three days, he would be engaged to be married. Of this, he had no doubt.

* * * *

Jacob sat at his desk, unable to concentrate. He sat there between meetings, swaying back and forth in the chair, tossing his lucky Titleist up and down, and up and down. He couldn't get last night off his mind.

Yesterday had been booked solid with meetings, as he and his leadership team continued implementing the transformation plan. Jacob sent everyone home early. He wanted to give them some of their own time back. After all, they had given him plenty of it in recent weeks. Once they were all gone, he locked up and he left, too. He wasn't going home. He was going for a walk.

With a cool breeze blowing off the Detroit River, Jacob maneuvered his way through the streets. He felt the warmth of the sun on his face and was lulled by the hum of cars passing by—a sign of a city on the move.

He walked down Renaissance Drive, across Atwater Street, to the Detroit Riverwalk where he found a bench.

He gazed across the river toward Canada, watching the sailboats and barges glide by. Tonight was the night. Tonight Joanna would be his forever. He smiled at the thought. It felt good.

Within a couple of hours, he was standing at the threshold of Joanna's apartment, the ring in the breast pocket of his suit coat. Reservations at The Whitney were confirmed—the same table at the same place as their first *official* date. When Joanna opened the door, she was wearing a knee-length purple dress with a gray sweater. Her hair was curled into beautiful blonde spirals. Jacob couldn't resist beaming. "Hi," was all he said, then gave her a kiss.

Jacob had arranged, with the help of the maitre'd, for a dozen red roses to be placed at Joanna's seat. She was caught off guard, and her face flooded with a red blush that brought a small tear to Jacob's eye. This woman had changed his life, and he couldn't wait any longer to make her his wife.

As the waiter brought two glasses of champagne, Jacob began, "Joanna, the night you stepped into my life, I was lost. Things were spinning nearly out of control for me then. But, from the moment you said your first words to me, everything changed. Over the last few months, every moment I have spent with you has been the best moment of my life."

He reached into his breast pocket, fell to one knee, and pulled out the little square box.

Jacob continued, "I want to make every day, for the rest of my life, the best day of my life. I can only do that if you are next to me, as my wife. Joanna, will you marry me?"

Her hands shot to her mouth and tears filled her eyes. She nodded, speechless. Jacob opened the box, revealing a stunning radiant-cut diamond on a diamond band. He was proud to have picked out the ring himself.

"Oh, Jacob," Joanna finally managed to speak, "it's beautiful."

"Um, you still haven't answered my question ..." he said, smiling.

"Of course, yes! I'll marry you! This is perfect," she said. She cupped his face in her hands and kissed him. He slipped the ring onto her finger.

The rest of the night went by in a flash. They talked about the wedding, on June 24, the same day her parents and her grandparents were married, places they could go for a honeymoon, and even how the business was going to factor into all of their personal plans. The only thing that truly mattered this night was their new future together.

Chapter 25: The Power Within

Be the change that you wish to see in the world.
- Gandhi

As Jacob rolled over the next morning, he was greeted by the smiling face of the woman he loved. Joanna had been up for a while, staring at the ring Jacob had given her the night before. Jacob could not have planned for a more perfect morning. He hated for it to end, but he needed to get going. He wasn't planning to go straight to work. He was stopping by Dr. Marc's office to share his good news.

Dr. Marc's office was unusually silent as he entered. There were no patients in the waiting room area, and the phones were quiet. Jacob hardly noticed. He did, however, notice that the receptionist was wiping her nose with a tissue, her eyes red from crying.

She looked at him and in a shaky voice, said, "I'm sorry, sir, we're not taking appointments today. Is there something I can help you with?"

Taken back by the look on her face, Jacob softly said, "I don't need an appointment, ma'am, I'm here to see Dr. Marc. Is he in?" Upon hearing Dr. Marc's name, the receptionist burst into tears. And then Jacob knew.

"I am so sorry," she said, as she wiped her eyes. "Dr. Marc passed away unexpectedly yesterday. He had a pain in his stomach, was rushed to the ER and passed away a few hours later. We are all in shock."

Jacob's heart hit the floor. There was no way this was possible! He had just talked to Dr. Marc on the phone a few days ago. It could not be. It simply could not be.

The receptionist broke Jacob's train of thought, "What did you say your name was?"

"I, uh, I hadn't given my name. I'm sorry. I'm Jacob Wengrow. I was coming to talk to Dr. Marc. He's been helping me for the last couple of months. I wanted to surprise him today," Jacob said, fighting back the tears of his own.

"Jacob? Of course. I remember you, sorry about that. Dr. Marc talked about you all the time. Oh boy, he sure did love his talks with you. I have something for you. Dr. Marc was telling me how much he enjoyed your talk the other day and he had written you a personal note, that he had asked me to mail."

She went to his office and found the letter on Dr. Marc's desk that was ready to be mailed to Jacob. She held out the white envelope with his name scribbled across it. Jacob's hands began to tremble as he reached for the letter.

He sat down in the waiting area and carefully opened the envelope. He read,

Jacob,

After we had hung up the phone the other day, I was so excited to hear your "big news." First, let me say that I am so proud of you. For the short time we have known each other, you have been a constant encouragement to me. Watching you fight hard for the things you cared about gave me a renewed outlook on life. I know that it hasn't been easy, but I do know the struggles you have gone through—and will continue to go through—will make you that much stronger. I've been there, and I see a lot of myself in you. Keep chasing after everything you want out of this life. If I've learned one thing, it is that your time is short, so make the most out of it that you can.

Second, I have been reflecting on many of our talks and many of my own bucket list goals that I have not yet accomplished. You have inspired me to take on an associate and start slowing down a bit. I've only taken Wednesdays off for the last few decades. It isn't enough anymore. I wanted you to know that although you may have thought of yourself as the student, you in many ways were a

*teacher. It's time for me to golf in Florida during the winter
and travel to the places I've wanted to see. I've been
putting it off, waiting for the right time.*

*I wanted to thank you for teaching me to slow down,
reflect, and plan. I decided I've been at this too long, and I
want to chase some of my own dreams. I have loved every
second that I have been a dentist, but now, at my age, it's
time to move to a warmer climate, golf and fish awhile.
Thanks for pushing me to my next level. Whether you knew
it or not, you have been an equal influence on me and my
life.*

*This leads me to one last thing. There was something
that you didn't know or recognize about all of the advice I
gave you, Sam gave you, and everyone else gave you on
this journey. None of it meant anything if you first didn't
want the change. This has always been inside you: your
instinct, your ability, and your talents are what have made
all of this possible.*

*Please, whatever you do, never forget that everything
that you have been searching for and longing for has been
inside of you all along. You have always had the power to
make it happen. Always keep your action in motion, Jacob!*

*I love you like a son, Jacob. Keep fighting the good
fight.*

Looking forward to our next lunch!

Your good friend and mentor,
Dr. Marc

P.S. By the way, I don't even need to know what Joanna said, I know she said YES! Congrats. I can't wait to celebrate at your wedding!

Jacob folded the letter and returned it to the envelope. He couldn't move. He was completely numb. Sitting alone, the tears began to roll down his cheeks.

Dr. Marc had wanted to do so many things in his life but didn't have the chance. It was one final lesson from Dr. Marc. Jacob now recognized the importance of having balance in his life. Although he was driven and on the right path towards growing his company, he had to make time for himself, his family, and kids—yes, they would surely be on the horizon.

Balance. There is no such thing as waiting until it's a good time. This would become an integral part of Jacob's personal mantra for the rest of his life. Dr. Marc always worked hard; but, in hindsight, he could have made time for more play, more fun. More balance. He openly cried for several minutes, and then reached into his pocket for his phone and dialed Joanna's number. He needed her more than anything else at this moment. She was the only person he wanted to talk to.

Chapter 26: Leaving the Party When You're Having Fun

If your actions inspire others to dream more, learn more, do more and become more, you are a leader.
- John Quincy Adams, Sixth President of the United States

As the sun set, Jacob and his son relaxed on the back patio of their home, deep in conversation. Here, in this spot, countless memories were made over the last few decades, and millions of laughs were had. Family and friends gathered here to relax or share a meal. It was as much a part of the family as the people were.

"And that's how I grew the company and met your mom," Jacob concluded to his grown son, Oliver. Oliver had heard this story dozens of times in his life, and never tired of it.

"Thanks for sharing that story again, Dad. I always love hearing it."

"Oliver, I felt like I had to tell it again. You know, I'm celebrating my seventieth birthday tomorrow. It's time for me to slow down. The business was a small startup and now is a thriving company with two hundred twenty-two employees and thirteen offices. I had incredibly loyal partners that have built this business with me. I bought them out so they could retire. I had one exceptional mentor and business coach in Sam. Now, it's my turn to retire and enjoy the next chapter of my life with your mom traveling, spending time with my grandkids, just enjoying what I've built. You can grow the company from here.

"You have worked tirelessly to learn the business. Your fundamental knowledge and ability to connect with the employees, the leadership team, and the customers is admirable. I wish I had your talent when I was your age. Now I am going to step down and hand the keys over to you completely. Tomorrow, the office is throwing me a birthday-retirement party. I will give my final speech and thank them for their years of outstanding service. Then, the company is yours.

"I'm very proud of you, and I know you will grow it in your own way. I'm here to advise you when you need me, of course. I know you will be great, I have no worries about that, Oliver!" Jacob said, with all the pride in the world flooding his every word.

"Dad, I know we have been planning this for some time: the contracts, the agreements, the sale of the company. But, I can't believe this is happening. I will make you proud and continue your legacy. Thank you for having faith in me. I don't know how to begin to—"

"Son, I'm not worried about you one bit. I have every faith that you will do what needs to get done to accomplish your own dreams. The world is moving at such a fast pace right now, and it will only continue to move faster. I can't keep up with the technology, the disruptors, the new generations, or anything else that I once handled with ease. You are young. You have your thumb on the pulse of all that. Many CEOs or presidents of companies stay too long. I have always believed that you leave the party while you're still having fun. I'm still having fun, but I know in my gut that it's time to slow down and pass the baton.

"Oliver, in this process, you will have many victories and learn lessons. Promise me that you will learn from all of your mistakes, stay grounded, and never stop growing. Deal?" Jacob said.

"Deal," Oliver responded as they hugged, with tears in their eyes. "I love you, Son," said Jacob.

"I love you too, Dad," Oliver replied. Jacob reached into his pocket, took out an old golf ball and handed it to his son. "Here. It brought me plenty of luck over the years. I know there's still some left in there for you."

For more information on working with Jon

to grow your business big, very big,

please call 248.535.7796

Acknowledgements

Thank you Mom and Dad, Wendy and Marc Dwoskin, for guiding me with your wisdom and love. Dad, thank you for the Brian Tracy tapes when I was 18 and thank you for being an example of hard work, dedication and the importance of continual learning. Mom, thank you for the laughter and for teaching me the power of humor, unconditional love and for listening to my instincts.

Thank you, Grandpa Sam Wengrow, for teaching me to have grit and always having confidence in me.

Thank you, Aunt Deborah Berris, for giving me advice and being my second mom.

Thank you to my wife, Joanna, for always having confidence in every business move I make and for being the best friend, wife, and mother to our children anyone could ask for. I am lucky and grateful to have you in my life. Thank you for making me a better human being. I love that our hands fit.

Thank you to my kids, Jacob and Aria, who bring so much joy and light into my life. I love you more than you can imagine. Thank you for the smiles, laughter, and everything you teach me every day.

Thank you to my sister, Jacki Berris, for everything you do for our entire family.

Thank you to my sister-in-law, Jamie Garavaglia, for all the laughs we share together.

Thank you to my brother, Jeff, for making it through the rain with me.

Thank you to my in-laws, Jeffrey and Linda Serman, who always treated me as one of their own and taught me more than I can express.

Thank you to my entire extended family for your love, kindness, and support.

Thank you to my business coach, Jules Rappaport, who always had my back and helped me find my inner strength.

Thank you, Ilan Milch and Dr. Paul Kay, for your directness and guidance.

Thank you to my incredibly dynamic team who always put their 110 percent into everything they do for me on a daily basis: Kristian Price, Stacey Corso, Maria Kuechler, Nora Masopust and Tina Sarafian.

Thank you to my longtime friends: Frank Borman, Scott Fishman, Adam Carrick, Dan Ortman, and Dylan Siegel for your friendship, support, advice, and laughs.

Thank you to all the teachers I have had along the way for putting up the much-needed mirror so I could grow on so many levels.

A special thank you to my co-writer, A.J. Reilly, without whom I could not have tackled this book. Thank you for your dedication, friendship, and helping to turn my vision into a story that I hope will help many.

Thank you to Brian Tracy, Anthony Robbins, Jim Rohn, and Ken Blanchard for getting me started on my journey. Thank you for sharing your wisdom, knowledge, and advice with me and the world.

Thank you to Barbara Terry and Waldorf Publishing for finding me, having faith in me and trusting me to be part of the Waldorf family.

Also, I would like to thank God for His guidance, direction, strengths, and gifts He provides me on a daily basis.

And, thank you to you, the reader, for picking up this book. May it bring you continued growth in your own journey, as it did for me.

Thank you, and remember always to Think Big!

Author Bio

If ever there was someone who wasn't interested in talking about himself, it's me. But, I know that you are wondering what makes me the expert I say that I am. Well, here it is. I recently turned forty-three and am excited to say that I have finally made a career out of being myself. I am an executive advisor, business coach, and founder/chief executive officer of The Jon Dwoskin Experience. I grow businesses big. **Very Big.**

When I was eighteen, my dad gave me Brian Tracy's audiotape series called *The Psychology of Success*. My dad said, "I know you'll do well in college, but I think you will get more out of these tapes than you will school." At that moment, my car became a university on wheels, and my Walkman a mobile classroom. I became obsessed with self-learning. I have spent every day since then studying business, life, and how to grow.

When I was twenty-one, I attended a Billy Joel-Elton John concert. I remember one moment when both artists came onstage and the entire audience erupted. I had a voice inside me saying, one day you will fill this arena with your words and you will inspire others. I always knew this was my calling, my purpose, my passion.

Something remarkable and life-altering happened to me when I was thirty-one. I realized that the way I was learning and recalling was unusual. I was tested and learned that I was dyslexic. It was second nature for me to figure out different ways to learn and problem solve outside the box.

Upon hearing the diagnosis, I set out on a mission to fully understand how I learn, thus providing a deep insight into how other people learn. I began to master this strategy in order to become more effective in business and in my personal life. It gave me mental clarity and the ability to understand not only how I learn but how to morph my creative thinking with my business thinking and to apply it in my success with growing businesses, companies and, most importantly, myself. I had no choice but to figure out the right and wrong ways of learning and growing for myself. And this now helps me grow others. **I have made a career out of my passion.** I understand how the businessperson functions, and the tools each one needs to grow not only their art, but the business of their organization. I've turned this passion into a career as a specialist in growing business big. Very Big!

My goals were not achieved without some challenges. When I was thirty and unsure of my next steps, I was diagnosed with testicular cancer. I remember thinking that from this point forward in my life, I was always going to follow my heart. Life is just too short and I vowed to not only live it, but to do my part to make it a better place for as many people as possible. Having been recently married and with thoughts of starting a family, this diagnosis was nothing short of terrifying. I underwent seventeen radiation treatments and regular checkups for the first five years, plus yearly checkups for an additional five years.

At my ten-year checkup, the doctor told me the cancer had returned and was riddled throughout my entire body. He said he had NO good news for me. He also said that he had never seen a case this bad in the history of his career. Around the corner, I would be facing chemo and, most likely, death.

I begged him to retake my blood. I needed both of us to be absolutely certain. He agreed to a new blood sample, but emergency CAT scans, ultrasounds, and follow-up appointments were arranged. For forty-eight hours, I was certain that I was dying.

My wife and I were at Starbucks when my doctor called with the results. He said, "Jon, you were right. They messed up the test. All your tests came back fine. You are fine. Go live your life."

My wife and I broke down crying. At this very moment, my fear of death was wiped away and a new perspective was made clear to me. I embarked on an aggressive search to get in alignment with my soul.

In Gary Zukav's book, *The Seat of the Soul,* he discusses the idea that the ideal human being cannot tell where their personality ends and their soul begins. I remember at this moment feeling just how out of alignment I was. I refreshed my quest for learning and personal growth to get back into alignment and make a career out of bringing the best out of people and helping them achieve their goals and live a better, more balanced, fun life. I had a taste of what it was like to face the end of life and I had a second chance. It was my rebirth. It was my time to be authentic. And this is the path I chose. I will be the first to tell you what I am not good at. But, I am good at many things.

This one thing is very true and comes intuitively to me: **I have the ability to see what is not being seen, hear what is not being heard and ask questions that are not being asked.** In short, I provide critical guidance needed for making the next pivotal business decision. I am a go-to solution expert who businesspeople turn to for advice, high-level strategy, and accountability, to grow their companies and achieve their own personal growth.

I'm not a "corporate" guy, but I learned a lot and played the game to win at a high degree ... and loved it all. Every day in corporate life came with valuable lessons, and for that I am grateful. I'm also grateful for this chance to return to my entrepreneurial roots. It really seemed like it was never going to happen. But, with courage, the proper advisors around me, a lot of faith, and a great wife supporting me, I made the leap. Go big, or go home! (Easier said than done.)

And, yes, I have had a successful professional career. I was recently the chief operating officer of The Hayman Company and led the firm in its restructuring. Previously, I was a vice president of investments with Marcus & Millichap, specializing in negotiating the sales of multi-family investment properties. After selling nearly five thousand units valued at nearly 250 million dollars, I was named the regional manager of the Detroit Marcus & Millichap office. I took over the office in August, 2008, and the recession that followed nearly obliterated us all the following month.

Despite the toll that the recession took, I successfully oversaw over four billion dollars in investment commercial transactions, building the Detroit office into the most profitable office of seventy-six offices nationwide. I expanded the office to forty-five agents by actively working with them to grow their agent teams and increase their bottom lines. I strategized, trained, and improved their skill sets and held them accountable to their business plans. I was a regional and national trainer, assisted in turning around offices, and was part of the CEO Advisory Committee. At that point, six years had passed and I knew it was time to move on.

That chapter was complete for me. Before my successful career in real estate, I created one of the first online marketing companies in the United States. This was one of the first times I remember tuning in to my instincts. The internet didn't exist, yet I knew it was going to be huge. Many people thought we were crazy, but I knew we were onto something new, uncharted and very big. It was 1995. I was twenty-three years old and leading the sales team. I sold the company in 1997 to USWeb, the largest internet professional service firm in the world. My brother

and I, along with a friend, started this in our parents'
basement, working one hundred-hour weeks for years.

**Being part of the Silicon Valley Boom was
phenomenal, but looking back, I wish I took more time
to breathe it all in.** Everything was moving so fast; I was
so young. And I loved every second of it. I'm honored to
have been awarded the prestigious Crain's "40 Under 40"
award and to have been an Eastern Michigan University
Alumnus of the Year Award recipient, having graduated
from there with a double major in Economics and
Journalism.

Through it all, I have always had business coaches –
as an agent, as a manager, always. Even before I knew
about "coaching," I had advisors whom I could turn to for
advice and inspiration to support and fuel the drive I had
within me. At times, I have had two coaches. It's true! In
fact, I currently have two coaches and use co-coaching with
other coaches in the industry.

It is through coaching that I found my voice, especially
when I took over at Marcus & Millichap. I learned how to
more effectively communicate with all the different agents,
both locally and nationally, and how to work with and
communicate more effectively with the C-level people of
the company. I continue to use coaches because they hold
me accountable and facilitate my own growth. After all,
even us coaches have dreams and aspirations!

I have a big heart and a long history of giving back. I have sat on the board of directors of nearly a dozen organizations in the past twenty years, served as a mentor to many, and continue to do so as my way of giving back and paying it forward.

I want to share one more important thought with you. As a cancer survivor, I am a mentor with Imerman Angels (imermanangels.org). I am a thirteen-year cancer survivor (and counting!) with every intention of staying that way. I mentor men who are, unfortunately, going through a very scary experience. If you or someone you know are in need of support, please email me and know that I will be there for you in a heartbeat. When I was going through my own diagnosis and treatment, my mentor was Jonny Imerman. His support was life-changing for me. That is why 1 percent of all profits from The Jon Dwoskin Experience goes to Imerman Angels, a one-on-one cancer support community.

Last, I want to tell you that I have a personal life. I live in a suburb of Detroit, Michigan, with my wife, Joanna, who makes true the old saying that behind every strong man is a stronger woman. She is a nurse and Reiki energy healer when she is not driving carpools, supervising homework, making meals, and raising our kids—all of which she does selflessly. Our son, Jacob, is an awesome basketball and tennis player with a kind heart. Our daughter, Aria, is an amazing singer, dancer, and pianist with a heart every bit as kind as her brother's. When I'm not busy growing businesses or guiding people through their next endeavors, I am playing tennis or basketball with friends or the kids, skiing, golfing, reading or listening to books, writing, or focusing on self-development.

About the Co-Author

A.J. Reilly was born near Detroit, Michigan, to a stay-at-home mom and a Baptist minister. Growing up he was heavily involved in athletics, earning a scholarship to play football in college. After college A.J. began to write, starting in 2014, after the death of his grandfather. A.J. teaches U.S. history in Plano, Texas, and signed his first publishing contract with Waldorf Publishing in 2015. He runs his own blog at storiesandstogies.com and most nights after school he is busy enjoying a fine cigar and pursuing his passion of writing.

CPSIA information can be obtained
at www.ICGtesting.com
Printed in the USA
FSHW011638021120
75403FS